God's building project

Nehemiah

by Eric Mason

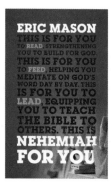

Nehemiah For You

If you are reading *Nehemiah For You* alongside this Good Book Guide, here is how the studies in this booklet link to the chapters of *Nehemiah For You*:

Study One → Ch 1-2   Study Five → Ch 6
Study Two → Ch 2-3   Study Six → Ch 6-7
Study Three → Ch 3-4   Study Seven → Ch 8-9
Study Four → Ch 5   Study Eight → Ch 10

Find out more about *Nehemiah For You* at:
www.thegoodbook.com/for-you

God's building project
The Good Book Guide to Nehemiah
© Eric Mason/The Good Book Company, 2022.
Series Consultants: Tim Chester, Tim Thornborough,
                    Anne Woodcock, Carl Laferton

Published by:
The Good Book Company

thegoodbook.com | thegoodbook.co.uk
thegoodbook.com.au | thegoodbook.co.nz | thegoodbook.co.in

Published in association with the literary agency of Wolgemuth & Associates.

ISBN: 9781784986773 | Printed in Turkey

CONTENTS

Introduction: Good Book Guides

Every Bible-study group is different—yours may take place in a church building, in a home or in a cafe, on a train, over a leisurely mid-morning coffee or squashed into a 30-minute lunch break. Your group may include new Christians, mature Christians, non-Christians, moms and tots, students, businessmen or teens. That's why we've designed these *Good Book Guides* to be flexible for use in many different situations.

Our aim in each session is to uncover the meaning of a passage, and see how it fits into the "big picture" of the Bible. But that can never be the end. We also need to appropriately apply what we have discovered to our lives. Let's take a look at what is included:

⊕ **Talkabout:** Most groups need to "break the ice" at the beginning of a session, and here's the question that will do that. It's designed to get people talking around a subject that will be covered in the course of the Bible study.

⊕ **Investigate:** The Bible text for each session is broken up into manageable chunks, with questions that aim to help you understand what the passage is about. The **Leader's Guide** contains **guidance for questions**, and sometimes ⊗ additional "follow-up" questions.

⊙ **Explore more (optional):** These questions will help you connect what you have learnedto other parts of the Bible, so you can begin to fit it all together like a jig-saw; or occasionally look at a part of the passage that's not dealt with in detail in the main study.

⊖ **Apply:** As you go through a Bible study, you'll keep coming across **apply** sections. These are questions to get the group discussing what the Bible teaching means in practice for you and, your church. ⊡ **Getting personal** is an opportunity for you to think, plan and pray about the changes that you personally may need to make as a result of what you have learned.

⊕ **Pray:** We want to encourage prayer that is rooted in God's word—in line with his concerns, purposes, and promises. So each session ends with an opportunity to review the truths and challenges highlighted by the Bible study, and turn them into prayers of request and thanksgiving.

The **Leader's Guide** and introduction provide historical background information, explanations of the Bible texts for each session, ideas for **optional extra** activities, and guidance on how best to help people uncover the truths of God's word.

Why study Nehemiah?

Nehemiah tells the story of the rebuilding of the walls of Jerusalem. God's people had been in captivity, but God had intervened so that they were allowed to come back to their own land and rebuild their broken city. It's a key moment in the history of God's people.

But we won't walk away from this book with just a rebuilt wall. There are far more riches than that in these pages!

Jerusalem was supposed to be a city on a hill, a light to the world, a representation of the rule of God. But its people had forgotten this. So the book of Nehemiah shows us the work it takes to rebuild representation of the glory of God. Nehemiah doesn't just rebuild the city walls; he rebuilds the social and spiritual character of the people, too. He deals with justice issues, resists the distractions of enemies, and reinstates the word of God in its place at the center of the life of the city.

This story has an obvious relevance to any type of rebuilding we might do for God—from our homes and families to our local churches, communities, cities, and government. It teaches us about gospel mission. It shows how, even in the midst of great need, opposition, rebellion, encumbrances, and sins, God still works through his people and motivates us to complete his work.

Only a few generations after Nehemiah, the Savior would come. Jesus would live, die, and rise again, and would guide the people of God—including you and me—beyond the walls of Jerusalem in mission, to establish his reign over the nations. It's with that perspective that we read the book of Nehemiah today.

We can see ourselves and our lives in the book of Nehemiah. But most of all we can see God's intentions, his glory, and his Son.

1 Nehemiah 1:1 – 2:8
REDEEMED TO REPRESENT

⊕ talkabout

1. Imagine the capital city of your country, or the place where you live, has been destroyed. How would you feel? What would you do?

⊕ investigate

▶ **Read Nehemiah 1:1-10.**

The Israelites had been in exile—scattered far from their homeland. But God had intervened and the people had begun to be allowed to go back to Jerusalem. At the start of the book of Nehemiah, some exiles have already returned, while others remain in Persia.

2. Among those who have already returned is Hanani, the brother of Nehemiah. What does he say about the state of Jerusalem (v 3)?

• What is Nehemiah's immediate reaction to the news (v 4)?

3. How does Nehemiah address God (v 5)?

• How do you think that might have helped him to pray?

4. What's the contrast between God and the people (v 5, 6-7)?

5. What did God say he would do if the people were unfaithful (v 8)?

• But what promise is Nehemiah hoping he will fulfill now (v 9)?

Jerusalem was the place where God had chosen to make his name dwell (v 9). It was the center of the whole nation, the center of their worship. It was the place where God's people were supposed to represent God's reign to the nations around them.

6. What has God done for his people that makes this possible (v 9, 10)?

Today we are the people who represent God to the world, wherever we are. He has redeemed us and is dwelling in us. He is rebuilding us into a better reflection of himself.

⊡ explore more

Jesus compares his followers to a city in Matthew 5:14: "You are the light of the world. A city set on a hill cannot be hidden." The church today is like Jerusalem. That's why Revelation 21 talks about a new, future Jerusalem.

> **Read Revelation 21:1-4**

What does the new Jerusalem have in common with the old Jerusalem (v 3)?

But what makes it better (v 4)?

The new Jerusalem is the community that every community is ultimately supposed to look like. And God wants us to be like movie trailers for that city. We want to be a reflection of the beauty of the new Jerusalem—and to see the gospel rebuild the lives of those around us, too.

⊡ getting personal

How does Nehemiah's passionate concern for the faithful representation of God challenge you personally? What would it look like in your life to care as much as Nehemiah does about obeying God and making his name known?

⊡ apply

7. What do you think it looks like for us to represent God's rule today?

• Where do you see brokenness in the representation of God's rule today? What will you ask him to rebuild?

⊙ investigate

▶ Read Nehemiah 1:11 – 2:8

After praying and fasting for four months (from Chislev, which is our November and December, to Nisan, which is our March and April), Nehemiah is finally ready to take action.

8. How does Nehemiah's conversation with the king begin (2:1-2)?

DICTIONARY

Nisan (2:1): a month in the Hebrew calendar, corresponding to our March and April.
Artaxerxes (v 1): the king of Persia.
The province Beyond the River (v 7): the part of the Persian Empire which lay west of the River Euphrates.

9. In verses 4-8, how do we see Nehemiah's dependence on the Lord?

• How do we see his own hard work and initiative?

10. What does the king grant Nehemiah?

• Why?

Nehemiah's interaction with the king is a case study in how to speak to unbelievers. He speaks with respect; he has prepared his request; he contextualizes what he says so that it makes sense to the king (who wouldn't understand about Jerusalem being God's city, but who would care about family legacy). And he is ready—he is willing to take any opportunity for God's glory.

⮕ apply

11. How can we use Nehemiah's example in our own conversations with unbelievers?

12. What do Nehemiah's actions throughout 1:1 – 2:8 teach us about what it looks like to prepare to represent God's rule to those around us?

• How can we put these things into practice today?

↑ pray

Spend some time in prayer for yourselves, your church, and the worldwide body of Christ. Thank God for redeeming you in Christ. Ask for his help and guidance in representing his reign to the world.

2 Nehemiah 2:9 – 3:32
BUILDING A TEAM

The story so far

When Nehemiah heard about the brokenness of Jerusalem, he wept. Then he prayed. Finally he went to the king and agreed a plan to rebuild the walls.

⊕ talkabout

1. What do you think holds people back from joining in with the ministries or missional work of their church?

⊕ investigate

> **Read Nehemiah 2:9-17**

2. Why does Nehemiah's request for letters of recommendation (see v 7-8) prove to be wise (v 10)?

> **DICTIONARY**
>
> **Derision (v 17):** mockery.

3. In verses 11-16, how else does Nehemiah show caution?

4. How does he describe his plans (v 12)?

Nehemiah has utter confidence in his vision. At the same time, he knows he needs to test his plans before sharing them. He stays quiet until he can make himself aware of the precise situation in Jerusalem.

5. When he does speak to the people, how does Nehemiah describe the problems in Jerusalem (v 17)?

- Why do you think he uses the words "we" and "us"?

Nehemiah is a pointer to Jesus here. Jesus left the right hand of God and made himself one of us, for our sake. Our own ministry should be like this too. Each of us was put where we are to help and develop others, and not to look down on them. Romans 12:15-16 urges us, "Rejoice with those who rejoice, weep with those who weep. Live in harmony with one another. Do not be haughty, but associate with the lowly." We own one another's problems, just like Nehemiah owned the problems in Jerusalem.

⊡ apply

6. In your church or small group, how could you promote a culture of helping one another and identifying with one another and those around you?

⊡ getting personal

Who do you know who is in trouble or suffering derision—perhaps because of their faith? What could you do to help, support, or encourage them?

⊡ investigate

▶ Read Nehemiah 2:19 – 3:2 (and, if you have time, skim-read all of 3:1-32)

7. How does Nehemiah encourage the people to get on board with his plans (2:18)?

> **DICTIONARY**
>
> **Portion (2:20):** possession or inheritance.
> **Consecrate (3:1):** mark out as holy.
> **Cubit (v 13):** the length of a forearm.

• How does he describe them (v 20)?

8. Why do you think Nehemiah's words encourage a sense of unity?

9. What's Nehemiah's attitude to those who don't agree with his plans?

10. What groups of people do we see working on the wall (3:1, 8, 9, 12)?

- Who would be the equivalent groups of people today? Can you imagine them all working together on a building project?

⊡ explore more

The first group we see building the wall is the priests (v 1)—even the high priest. This was a uniquely high role: the high priest was the person responsible for representing the people before God. And he is the one who first puts his hand to the plough. These priests are the spiritual leaders, and that means they want to set the tone for the community. When a leader serves, it motivates the rest of the people to serve, too.

1 Peter 2:9 describes Christians as "a royal priesthood." This means that the church is the servant leader of any community. We are all priests. Our role is to serve the people around us, lead them to God, and bring restoration.

▶ **Read 1 Peter 2:9**

What does Peter say is the point of being a royal priesthood?

How can the church take a lead in serving our communities today?

It's easy to think that the church only needs people of a certain type. But this passage illustrates the fact that we need people from all walks of life. We can all be active workers for God.

Spend some time reflecting on how you could leverage your particular background or situation for God. What personality traits and opportunities has he given you? Who has he put around you? What is one thing you could do to actively serve him this week?

11. Nehemiah's rebuilding project is all going to plan. Why do you think that is?

⊖ **apply**

12. What lessons can be learned from this passage today by...
  • those in leadership?

  • those who are part of a team running a ministry?

  • those who feel they can't serve, or don't know how?

⊡ getting personal

Think about any ministries you are part of, or would like to be part of. How could you personally put into practice Nehemiah's careful planning, or the people's willingness and sense of unity?

⊡ pray

Pray for the mission of your church. Pray for your leaders. Then ask God to unify the church as a whole, so that every person is able and willing to take part, for his glory.

3 Nehemiah 4:1-23
DEVELOPMENT AND DEFENSE

The story so far

When Nehemiah heard about the brokenness of Jerusalem, he wept. Then he prayed. Finally he went to the king and agreed a plan to rebuild the walls.

Nehemiah surveyed the city secretly, then called the people together to share his vision. Many different people joined in God's rebuilding project.

⊕ talkabout

1. What opposition might Christians face today and why?

⊕ investigate

▶ Read Nehemiah 4:1-9

2. What do Sanballat and Tobiah say about the rebuilding project (v 2-3)?

> **DICTIONARY**
>
> **Samaria (v 2):** the region north of Judah.
> **Arabs, Ammonites, Ashdodites (v 7):** people living to the south, east, and west of Judah.

• Why do you think they say these things?

3. Nehemiah responds by venting in prayer. What does he ask God to do (v 4-5)?

• What action does he take (v 6)?

4. How do you think Nehemiah felt at this point?

• What about the other builders (v 6)?

5. How does the opposition intensify (v 7-8)?

• How do Nehemiah and the people respond?

➔ apply

6. What does all this teach us about how to deal with opposition to God's work today?

⊡ explore more

optional

Our benchmark for how to respond to opposition is Jesus Christ.

▶ Read 1 Peter 2:21-23

What did Jesus do to those who threatened and mocked him?

How do we see Nehemiah doing the same? What does he do as a way of "entrusting himself to him who judges justly"?

⊡ getting personal

What difficulties are you facing in your work for the Lord? What do you think is at the root of any opposition? How can you respond wisely, following in Nehemiah's footsteps?

⊻ investigate

▶ Read Nehemiah 4:10-23

7. What further discouragements do the builders face (v 10-12)?

8. How does Nehemiah encourage them (v 14)?

• What's the result (v 15)?

9. What is Nehemiah's new strategy for making sure the building continues?
• v 16

• v 17-18

• v 19-20

● v 21

● v 22-23

10. The trumpet will call them all together to fight—but what's an even better thing to rally around (v 20)?

The people didn't just put on war clothes and strap swords to their sides. They understood that God was the one that would actually do the fighting. Even when they threw out their arms to fight, it was really God's arm over theirs. And, in fact, he had already frustrated their enemies' plans. Today, we're fighting for the cause of Christ. That makes the battle so much easier—because we're not fighting *for* victory but *from* victory. Jesus has already won.

11. In what ways does God fight for us…
● in the person of Jesus (see Colossians 2:15; Romans 8:34)?

• in the person of the Holy Spirit (see Ephesians 1:13-14; 6:17; Galatians 5:22-23)?

⮕ apply

12. Nehemiah calls the people to fight for their brothers (i.e., their fellow Jews), their sons and daughters, and their wives (v 14). What will it look like for us to do this today—fighting for God's glory in our lives and others'?

⊡ getting personal

The New Testament urges us to make every effort to build one another up (Romans 14:19), to maintain the unity of the Spirit (Ephesians 4:3), to pursue holiness (Hebrews 12:14; 2 Peter 3:14), and to stick to our faith (2 Peter 1:10). What could you do to work hard at these things—fighting for your faith and for the faith of those around you?

⬆ pray

Pray for those you know of who are facing opposition and hardship as they seek to build God's kingdom.

4 Nehemiah 5:1-19
WALKING IN THE FEAR OF GOD

The story so far

Jerusalem was broken down and Nehemiah made plans to rebuild its walls. Many different people joined in God's rebuilding project.

As the work progressed, they met with opposition from the surrounding peoples. But they were ready to fight, and they kept on building.

⊕ talkabout

1. What are some causes of injustice we see in the world today?

⊕ investigate

▶ **Read Nehemiah 5:1-13**

2. What must people do to get food (v 3)?

> **DICTIONARY**
>
> **Exacting (v 7):** demanding, forcing.

• What else are they being forced to do (v 4, 5)?

It isn't the pagans who are oppressing the poor in Jerusalem. It's the so-called religious people: "the Jewish brothers" (v 1). It's coming from within the community.

3. How does Nehemiah feel when he hears about this (v 6)?

• What two charges does he bring against the nobles and officials (v 7, 8)?

4. Nehemiah sums up what they are doing as not walking in the fear of God (v 9). Why do you think "fear of God" is at the root of acting justly?

5. What is Nehemiah's solution (v 10-11)?

explore more

optional

In the end, of course, the answer to injustice is Jesus.

❯ **Read Luke 4:16-21**

What is Jesus' mission statement?

How did Nehemiah put this into practice?

How did Jesus put this into practice?

Nehemiah doesn't just guarantee justice and reparation for the poverty-stricken inhabitants of Jerusalem. He also gives the oppressors a second chance. He doesn't punish them but calls them to repent and make things right.

6. How does he urge them to take this second chance seriously (v 13)?

⊡ apply

7. What unjust situations do you see around you today?

• What will it look like to respond as Nehemiah did?

⊡ getting personal

What injustices do you see in the world around you? What could you do to call the perpetrators to repentance unto redress the wrongs?

What injustices have you yourself perpetrated or been complicit in? What can you do to repent and make reparations?

⊥ investigate

> ❯ **Read Nehemiah 5:14-19**

DICTIONARY

Shekels (v 15): about 2/5oz or 11g.

8. What right does Nehemiah have as governor (v 14-15)?

- Previous governors have abused that right (v 15), but Nehemiah decides not to use it at all. Why not (v 15, 18)?

9. What do he and his servants do instead of growing food (v 16)?

10. Nehemiah is not just paying for his own food—what does he pay for and who does this serve (v 17-18)?

In other words, Nehemiah bent over backward and sacrificed even what was his due to serve the people. We see Jesus in this—who "came not to be served but to serve, and to give his life as a ransom for many" (Mark 10:45); who not only took on himself the price we should have paid for sin but also welcomes us to eat with him at his own expense.

⊡ apply

11. Western culture has a philosophy of entitlement: we often talk about our rights or about what we deserve. How does this passage challenge that?

- What situations can you think of today where giving up our rights would be a way of serving others?

⊡ getting personal

What would it look like in your life this week to lay down your rights for the sake of others?

⊡ apply

12. Nehemiah exemplifies Micah 6:8: "What does the Lord require of you but to do justice, and to love kindness, and to walk humbly with your God?" Why do you think these things express "the fear of God"—the lordship of God in our lives?

- How can we put each of these things into practice?

⬆ pray

Jesus taught us to pray, "Your kingdom come, your will be done, on earth as it is in heaven" (Matthew 6:10). Spend time praying together for situations of injustice or oppression that you see in your own community and in the wider world. Ask God to rule in those situations. Ask him for his help in doing whatever you can to act in line with his will.

5 STAY FOCUSED

Nehemiah 6:1 – 7:4

The story so far

Nehemiah made plans to rebuild the broken walls of Jerusalem. Many different people joined in. They faced opposition but were ready to fight for God's work.

The next crisis involved economic oppression within the people. Nehemiah stood up for justice, called for repentance, and surrendered his own rights for others.

⊕ talkabout

1. "Focus matters. You can have all the abilities and opportunities in the world, but if you don't have focus, you'll never get anywhere." Do you agree? In what situations might this be true?

⊥ investigate

▶ Read Nehemiah 6:1-9

> **DICTIONARY**
>
> **Breach (v 1):** gap or break.
> **Hakkephirim in the plain of Ono (v 2):** a place to the north-west of Jerusalem.
> **An open letter (v 5):** a letter without a seal, which anyone can read.

☺ getting personal

What does it mean to you to focus on God? Is there some specific way of serving others that he is calling you to focus on for him?

2. What do Sanballat, Tobiah, and Geshem do first of all to try to take Nehemiah off focus (v 2-4)?

3. Why might Nehemiah be tempted to do what they want?

• Why doesn't he?

It is interesting that Nehemiah says "I cannot come down" (v 3). Ono is north-west of Jerusalem. Geographically, it's above where Nehemiah is. But to him, anything that is not God's will is always a step down.

4. What is God's enemies' next tactic (v 4-7)?

5. How would you have responded if you were Nehemiah?

• How does he actually respond (v 8)?

optional

⊡ explore more

Colossians 3 tells us what it means to stay focused for Christians today: "Seek the things that are above, where Christ is" (v 1).

▶ Read Colossians 3:3, 9-10

What makes it possible to "seek the things that are above"?

▶ Read Colossians 3:12-17

What do these verses tell us about what it means to "seek the things that are above"?

⊡ apply

6. What things today might seem reasonable or attractive but would stop us focusing on God or his mission?

• What negative or difficult things might take us off focus?

How does Nehemiah stay focused? He prays, "O God, strengthen my hands" (v 9). It's like saying, "I want to remain focused. I don't want anything to get in the way of what you have called me to do." That's a prayer we can all pray every day.

⊡ investigate

❯ Read Nehemiah 6:10 – 7:4

7. Shemaiah claims to have a prophecy from the Lord for Nehemiah. But where does it really come from (6:10-13)?

DICTIONARY

Prophecy (v 12): a message (supposedly) from God.
Elul (v 15): a month in the Hebrew calendar, corresponding to our August and September.

• How does Nehemiah know it cannot come from God?

8. How do you think Nehemiah's prayer in verse 14 helps him to stay focused on the task at hand?

9. How do people in the surrounding nations respond to the completion of the walls (v 16)?

- Why do you think their understanding of what has happened leads to this response?

10. What has taken the nobles of Judah off focus (v 18-19)?

- What do they do as a result (v 17, 19)?

11. What two things does Nehemiah do to maintain focus after the walls are finished (7:2, 3)?

⊡ **apply**

12. What can we learn from Nehemiah about how to remain focused on God and his mission? How can we put these things into practice?

⊡ **getting personal**

What could tempt you off focus? How can you stay focused on God and his mission?

⬆ **pray**

Pray in line with Nehemiah's prayers. Ask him to strengthen your hands (6:9) in whatever he has called you to do. And ask him to deal with any opposition or difficulty (v 14) so that you don't get afraid or distracted. Praise God that he is the one who accomplishes his work through us (v 16).

6 REBUILT THROUGH THE WORD

The story so far

Nehemiah made plans to rebuild the broken walls of Jerusalem. Many different people joined in. They faced opposition but were ready to fight for God's work.

The next crisis involved economic oppression within the people. Nehemiah stood up for justice, called for repentance, and surrendered his own rights for others.

Despite his enemies' efforts to distract or harm him, Nehemiah remained focused on God's work, and the wall was finished.

⊕ talkabout

1. How do you find reading God's word? What do you like about it? What is hard?

In chapter 7, Nehemiah takes an inventory of all God's people. He is getting ready to assemble everyone together (v 5). We're seeing community formation: Nehemiah wants to know who is a member and who's just an attender. Who is actually ready to represent God's reign?

In chapter 8 this newly defined community is ready to assemble all together in one place.

⊕ investigate

▶ **Read Nehemiah 8:1-8**

DICTIONARY

Levites (v 7): temple servants.

2. Who comes together and why (v 1-2)?

3. How long do they listen for (v 3)?

4. What measures are taken to make sure people can clearly hear and understand (v 4, 7-8)?

5. How do they respond to what they hear (v 5-6)?

→ **apply**

6. Do you think Christians today share this reverence for God's word? Why, or why not?

7. What could be some ways of showing a right attitude toward God's word as we gather as Christians?

• What about in our personal reading of the Bible?

⊡ getting personal

What help do you need to understand God's word clearly? Is there someone you could ask for help when you find it hard? What resources could you take advantage of? What could you do to help others to understand? Decide on two practical steps forward you will take this week.

⊡ investigate

> **Read Nehemiah 8:9-18**

8. Why do you think the people respond the way they do as they hear the Law (v 9)?

DICTIONARY

Moses (v 14): the leader of God's people at the time of the exodus. He received the Law from God.
Booths (v 14): temporary shelters.
Jeshua (v 17): Joshua, the leader of God's people after Moses.

• But what are they told to do (v 9-12)?

This is a day when God is giving a new start to the people of Israel. So they can rejoice in him instead of grieving about themselves.

⊡ **getting personal**

The joy of the Lord means being satisfied in the Lord. This is what gives us strength.

In what area of your life do you need that spiritual strength? How can you turn to God to find it? Ask for his help in finding joy in him.

9. Who comes back for more the following day (v 13)?

10. Why do they build leafy booths (v 14-17)?

• Why do you think they rejoice so much at this (v 17)?

The people are celebrating the Feast of Booths or Tabernacles. Leviticus 23 contains the instructions for this festival.

> ❯ **Read Leviticus 23:42-43**

What are the people supposed to remember?

The festival points to Israel's new birth as a nation. It was a way of recognizing what God had delivered them from and the fact that he provided for them and remained faithful to them through the wilderness.

What particular significance do you think this would have had for the people in Nehemiah's time?

11. Why do you think the people are so desperate to saturate themselves in God's word?

In this passage, the people weep, rejoice, and commit themselves to God—all as a result of reading God's word and allowing it to form them as a community. It's worth thinking through how we could allow our own church communities to be formed by Scripture in this way.

⊟ **apply**

12. What can we do to maintain habits of paying attention to God's word, and then putting it into practice? How can we help each other with this?

⊡ pray

Spend some time worshiping God together. Praise him for his word.
Praise him that Jesus' perfect obedience to God's Law is credited to us
as his followers, even when we don't measure up in our own actions.
Pray for one another, that you would be formed by God's word both as a
community and individually.

7 SACRIFICIAL COMMITMENT

The story so far

Nehemiah made plans to rebuild the broken walls of Jerusalem. Many different people joined in. They faced opposition but were ready to fight for God's work.

Seeing economic oppression, Nehemiah stood up for justice among the people. He remained focused despite distractions and the wall was finished.

Nehemiah assembled all the people and recorded who they were. Together they read God's word and responded to it with prayer, joy, and action.

⊕ talkabout

1. Why do couples make promises to one another when they get married?

⊕ investigate

❯ Read Nehemiah 9:1-38

DICTIONARY

Sackcloth (v 1): very rough, itchy fabric, worn to express grief.
Iniquities (v 2): sins.
Host (v 6): a large number of people or things.
Abram/Abraham (v 7): the ancestor of the Israelites.
Ur of the Chaldeans (v 7): an ancient city in what is now Iraq.
Canaanite, Hittite, Amorite, Perizzite, Jebusite, Girgashite (v 8): people groups which previously lived in the promised land.
Red Sea (v 9): a sea which the Israelites crossed miraculously in Exodus 14.

Pharaoh (v 10): the king of Egypt.
Mount Sinai (v 13): the mountain where Moses encountered God.
Statutes (v 13): laws.
Sabbath (v 14): a day of rest.
Presumptuously (v 16): arrogantly.
Abounding in (v 17): rich in, full of.
Forsake (v 17): abandon.
Manna (v 20): a special bread which God gave the Israelites as they traveled through the desert.
Fortified (v 25): well-defended.
Cistern (v 25): a hole in the ground dug for water-storage.
Dominion (v 28): power, rule.
Covenant (v 32): a binding agreement.

2. In the following verses, what do the Levites say about what God is like and what he's done?

- v 6

- v 7-8

- v 9-15

- v 17-21

- v 22-25

3. What about the people? What were they like and what did they do (v 16-18)?

4. What happened next, repeatedly (v 26, 27, 28, 29-30)?

• What was the culmination of this (v 30)?

5. What situation are the people in now (v 36-37)?

• What do they say about the situation God has put them in (v 33)? Do you agree with their judgment?

Verses 2-3 summarize everything we've just read: they "confessed their sins and the iniquities of their fathers … They made confession and worshiped the LORD their God." The people are wearing sackcloth and sprinkling dirt on their heads (v 1). The message is, *We're a mess, we're sinful, we're dirty, and we need some help.*

6. How do they conclude their prayer (v 38)?

• A covenant is an agreement to be faithful to God. Why do you think it was so important to recount all that history before they get to making this covenant?

⊡ getting personal

What would be your equivalent of the Levites' prayer? What sins would you confess? How would you recognize God's faithfulness?

⊖ apply

7. What strikes you the most about this record of God's dealings with his people? What will you say to him or what will you do as a result?

⊍ investigate

The people are making a major recommitment to God. 10:1-27 lists the names of those who sign the promises they are making. But verses 28-29 reveal that all the people—"all who have knowledge and understanding"—make these promises too.

▶ **Read Nehemiah 10:28-39**

They "enter into a curse and an oath" (v 29). This means saying, "I swear that I will do this. And if I don't, let me be cursed."

DICTIONARY

Forego (v 31): go without.
Showbread (v 33): special bread in the temple.
New moon (v 33): a type of festival.
Sin offering (v 33): a sacrifice to make amends for sin.
Atonement (v 33): making amends.
Firstfruits (v 35): the first part of a crop.
Tithe (v 37): ten percent of income.
Minister (v 39): serve.

⊡ getting personal

Curses held people accountable to the covenant. We still need that accountability! It can be helpful to make an intentional agreement with a friend you trust and admire and give them permission to rebuke you if you need it.

Who could do this for you?

8. What do they promise to do (v 29)?

9. In the promises in the following verses, what sacrifice are the people making, and/or what are they trusting God about?

• v 30

• v 31

• v 32-34

• v 35-37

• v 37-39

➔ apply

10. Because of Jesus, we don't have to make sacrifices to pay for our sin. But what does making sacrifices (whether of money, time, or something else) demonstrate about our attitude toward God?

11. How can we express commitment to and trust in God when it comes to…
   • our families?

   • our finances and work life?

• any other area of life?

⬇ investigate

Now that the people have committed themselves to the Lord, they have to get themselves organized. 11:1 – 12:26 is a list of who lived where in Jerusalem and the surrounding area, and who played what role. Once all this has been put in order, they are at last ready to celebrate the finished wall.

▶ Read Nehemiah 12:27-43 (or, if you are pushed for time, just verses 27 and 43)

It's a huge celebration. Everyone is there. Two choirs parade around the walls, meeting in the temple.

DICTIONARY

Netophathites (v 28): inhabitants of an area near Jerusalem.
Beth-gilgal, Geba, Azmaveth (v 29): places near Jerusalem.
David (v 36): the greatest king of Israel, who first made Jerusalem the capital.

12. In verse 43, what do they do to complete the dedication?

• What's the overall feeling here?

⬆ pray

Pray your own prayer of commitment and dedication to God. Pray that he would make you rejoice—and that your joy would be "heard far away" (v 43) by those who don't yet know him.

8 UNCOMPROMISED FAITH

The story so far

Under Nehemiah's leadership, the walls of Jerusalem were rebuilt. Nehemiah called people to fight for God's work, to stand up for justice, and to stay focused.

After the walls were finished, the people read God's word together and responded to it. They grieved past sins and recommitted themselves to God.

⊕ talkabout

1. When is compromise a good thing? When isn't it?

⊕ investigate

❯ Read Nehemiah 12:44 – 13:3

2. What gets organized in 12:44-47?

> **DICTIONARY**
>
> **Asaph (12:46):** a writer of many psalms.
> **Zerubbabel (v 47):** another leader who brought exiles back to Jerusalem.
> **Ammonite, Moabite (13:1):** people historically hostile to God.
> **Balaam (v 2):** a prophet (Numbers 22- 24).

• How does this good organization express worship and commitment?

3. How else do the people express their commitment to God (13:1-3)?

This should not be viewed as racial exclusivity. As always, foreigners could become part of Israel by conversion (Ezra 6:21; Ruth 1:13-17). But God is concerned about spiritual influence. Historically, the Moabite culture was fundamentally opposed to God. So only a Moabite who had left his or her own culture and become officially part of the Israelite people could be part of the assembly. God wanted his people to be fully committed to him.

But before all of this happened, we are told, something else took place which threatened the people's worship and commitment.

❯ Read Nehemiah 13:4-9

4. What has happened (v 4-5)?

DICTIONARY

Frankincense (v 5): a type of perfume.

• Why is this a bad thing?

5. When Nehemiah finds out about this, what does he do (v 7-9)?

God is the one who was supposed to dwell in the temple, not Tobiah! Today God dwells in us by his Spirit—but the devil wants us to forget that. If I am spending time on something that is not godly, I have got a Tobiah in my life. And that's bad news. We must not let anything take the place of God.

⊡ apply

6. What are some things that can be like Tobiah in our lives?

• What does it look like to deal with those things the way Nehemiah does?

As Christians we now know that it's the blood of Christ that cleanses us from our wrongdoing (1 John 1:7) and the Spirit who works in us to put us back in order (Galatians 5:16, 22-23). We can start afresh and live righteously with his help.

⊡ investigate

⊳ Read Nehemiah 13:10-31

7. Next, Nehemiah discovers that more commitments have been compromised. What are they (v 10, v 15-16, v 23)?

DICTIONARY

Tyrians (v 16): people from Tyre, a city on the coast.
Wrath (v 18): anger.
Profaning (v 18): treating something holy with disrespect.
Desecrate (v 29): treat something holy with disrespect.

8. Nehemiah says something about each of these things (v 11, 17-18, 25-27). What do his words reveal about his own motivations and heart?

⊡ **explore more**

optional

Solomon was beloved by God and was the wisest man who had ever lived (1 Kings 3:12). Yet even he fell into sin when his foreign wives led him astray.

▶ **Read 1 Kings 11:1-8**

Why did God tell his people not to marry foreigners (v 2)?

But why was Solomon tempted to disobey (v 2)?

How did it become clear that his faith was compromised (v 5-8)?

9. How does Nehemiah deal with each of these failures?
   • v 11-13

   • v 19-22

   • v 25

Verse 25 reveals the depth of Nehemiah's anger about the people's disobedience. He actually beat some of these men up! He is deeply upset that they have broken their oath. These men's children can't even understand the language of Judah—which means that they can't understand their Scriptures or join in properly with temple worship. So these marriages are a kind of treachery against God (v 27).

The Bible doesn't seem to judge the response of Nehemiah as good or bad—though it certainly doesn't encourage us to marry outside the faith. It is focusing more on Israel's actions. The key thing is not to compromise God's word for the sake of our personal preferences.

10. What do Nehemiah's prayers in verses 14 and 22 show about his motives? Who does he seek to please?

11. What final things does Nehemiah set right in verses 28-31?

God's people have a Tobiah in the temple—more than one. They have reneged on the commitments they made in chapter 10. Despite their joy at the dedication of the wall, and the covenant they agreed, they have slid into compromise. Yet there is hope. Nehemiah has called them back to their commitments again.

⊟ apply

12. What does it look like today to be uncompromising in our passion for the Lord?

⊡ getting personal

Who do you know who is a beacon of committed, uncompromised faith? Could you encourage them about the way you see God at work in them?

Who do you know who seems to be stumbling? Could you help them stand firm?

↑ pray

Look back at the lessons you have learned in reading Nehemiah. What have you learned about God that you want to praise him for? What commitments do you want to make as a result? Pray together for God's help in keeping those commitments and in representing his kingdom to the people around you, for his glory.

God's building project

project

LEADER'S GUIDE

Leader's Guide

INTRODUCTION

Leading a Bible study can be a bit like herding cats—everyone has a different idea of what the passage could be about, and a different line of enquiry that they want to pursue. But a good group leader is more than someone who just referees this kind of discussion. You will want to:

- correctly understand and handle the Bible passage. But also...

- encourage and train the people in your group to do this for themselves. Don't fall into the trap of spoon-feeding people by simply passing on the information in the Leader's Guide. Then...

- make sure that no Bible study is finished without everyone knowing how the passage is relevant for them. What changes do you all need to make in the light of the things you have been learning? And finally...

- encourage the group to turn all that has been learned and discussed into prayer.

Your Bible-study group is unique, and you are likely to know better than anyone the capabilities, backgrounds, and circumstances of the people you are leading. That's why we've designed these guides with a number of optional features. If they're a quiet bunch, you might want to spend longer on *talkabout*. If your time is limited, you can choose to skip *explore more*, or get people to look at these questions at home. Can't get enough of Bible study? Well, some studies have optional extra homework projects. As leader, you can adapt and select the material to the needs of your particular group.

So what's in the Leader's Guide? The main thing that this Leader's Guide will help you to do is to understand the major teaching points in the passage you are studying, and how to apply them. As well as guidance for the questions, the Leader's Guide for each session contains the following important sections:

THE BIG IDEA

One or two key sentences will give you the main point of the session. This is what you should be aiming to have fixed in people's minds as they leave the Bible study. And it's the point you need to head back toward when the discussion goes off at a tangent.

SUMMARY

An overview of the passage, including plenty of useful historical background information.

OPTIONAL EXTRA

Usually this is an introductory activity that ties in with the main theme of the Bible study, and is designed to "break the ice" at the beginning of a session. Or it may be a "homework project" that people can tackle during the week.

So let's take a look at the various different features of a Good Book Guide:

⊕ talkabout

Each session kicks off with a discussion question, based on the group's opinions or experiences. It's designed to get people talking and thinking in a general way about the main subject of the Bible study.

⬇ investigate

The first thing you and your group need to know is what the Bible passage is about, which is the purpose of these questions. But watch out—people may come up with answers based on their experiences or teaching they have heard in the past, without referring to the passage at all. It's amazing how often we can get through a Bible study without actually looking at the Bible! If you're stuck for an answer, the Leader's Guide contains guidance for questions. These are the answers to direct your group to. This information isn't meant to be read out to people—ideally, you want them to discover these answers from the Bible for themselves. Sometimes there are optional follow-up questions (see ⊻ in guidance for questions) to help you help your group get to the answer.

⬆ explore more

These questions generally point people to other relevant parts of the Bible. They are useful for helping your group to see how the passage fits into the "big picture" of the whole Bible. These sections are OPTIONAL—only use them if you have time. Remember that it's better to finish in good time having really grasped one big thing from the passage, than to try and cram everything in.

→ apply

We want to encourage you to spend more time working at application—too often, it is simply tacked on at the end. In the Good Book Guides, apply sections are mixed in with the investigate sections of the study. We hope that people will realize that application is not just an optional extra, but rather, the whole purpose of studying the

Bible. We do Bible study so that our lives can be changed by what we hear from God's word. If you skip the application, the Bible study hasn't achieved its purpose.

These questions draw out practical lessons that we can all learn from the Bible passage. You can review what has been learned so far, and think about practical differences that this should make in our churches and our lives. The group gets the opportunity to talk about what they personally have learned.

⊡ getting personal

These can be done at home, but it is well worth allowing a few moments of quiet reflection during the study for each person to think and pray about specific changes they need to make in their own lives. Why not have a time for reporting back at the beginning of the following session, so that everyone can be encouraged and challenged by one another to make application a priority?

⬆ pray

In Acts 4:25-30 the first Christians quoted Psalm 2 as they prayed in response to the persecution of the apostles by the Jewish religious leaders. Today however, it's not as common for Christians to base prayers on the truths of God's word as it once was. As a result, our prayers tend to be weak, superficial, and self-centered rather than bold, visionary, and God-centered.

The prayer section is based on what has been learned from the Bible passage. How different our prayer times would be if we were genuinely responding to what God has said to us through his word.

1 Nehemiah 1:1 – 2:8
REDEEMED TO REPRESENT

THE BIG IDEA
The opening of the book of Nehemiah shows us how to represent God's rule on earth: with passion, prayer, and careful planning!

SUMMARY
The Israelites had been in exile—scattered far from their homeland. But God had intervened and the people had begun to be allowed to go back to Jerusalem. Among those who have already returned to Jerusalem is Hanani, the brother of Nehemiah. He comes back to Susa, the capital of Persia, and comes to see his brother (v 1-2). He tells him that the walls of Jerusalem remain broken and that those who live there are in "great trouble and shame" (v 3). Nehemiah is brokenhearted and begins to fast and pray (v 4).

Before Nehemiah does anything else, he cries out to God. He starts by stating who God is. God is sovereign over all creation. But he also breaks into specific circumstances. So Nehemiah calls him "the great and awesome God," but also underlines God's loyal love to his people (v 5). Next he prays based on these characteristics. He confesses the people's comprehensive unfaithfulness to God (v 6-7). Then he prays God's word back to him: asking him to keep his promise not only to scatter the disobedient (which has already happened) but also to gather the people back to Jerusalem (v 8-9). This city is where God's name dwells—it is supposed to be the place where God's people represent his rule.

Nehemiah asks God to give him success as he asks the king for help (v 11). In chapter 2 we see him take action. Nehemiah is the king's cupbearer, and he decides to leverage that role. He is visibly sad, and explains why when Artaxerxes asks (2:1-3). His gentle, careful answer means that the king is ready to listen. "What are you requesting?" he says (v 4). Nehemiah now shows his dependence on God, going into a quick prayer for help before making his request (v 4). We see that he has made meticulous plans: he knows exactly what he needs from the king (v 5-8). The result is that Artaxerxes gives him everything he asks.

OPTIONAL EXTRA
Play a game in which one person has to represent another person without any preparation. Divide the group into pairs. Each pair has a "professor" and an "interpreter." The "professor" is an eminent foreign scientist who is presenting his or her new discovery or invention to the rest of the group. But there is a language barrier. While the "professor" mimes, the "interpreter" must give the verbal part of the presentation. No conferring beforehand! Inventions can be as creative as you like—try thinking of a new device for the kitchen, a new method of transport, or something that will revolutionize communications.

GUIDANCE FOR QUESTIONS
1. Imagine the capital city of your country, or the place where you live, has been destroyed. How would you feel? What would you do? When people's homes are destroyed, it's like you can see the rubble and dust in their eyes! They feel broken. That feeling can be even more

powerful when it's a place that represents something important—the way a capital city can represent the nation as a whole. We are about to see that, at the time of Nehemiah, Jerusalem had been destroyed and the people were distraught. But we'll also see in this study that Jerusalem represented something much bigger than just the nation of Israel.

2. Among those who have already returned is Hanani, the brother of Nehemiah. What does he say about the state of Jerusalem (v 3)? There is only a small group of people still left in the city. But this remnant is "in great trouble and shame" (v 3), and the wall of Jerusalem has been broken down. The city walls had been destroyed when the people first went into exile.

• **What is Nehemiah's immediate reaction to the news (v 4)?** He feels the same brokenness as the people in Jerusalem do. He weeps and mourns for days. But he also begins to cry out to God.

3. How does Nehemiah address God (v 5)? Nehemiah recognizes who God is: the God of heaven, great and awesome (the word "great" is not a throwaway word but means "important"; the word "awesome" points to the idea of standing in awe of God, fearing his power and might). But God is not only all-powerful but also loving. He "keeps covenant and steadfast love." God is more loyal than a mother. He has chosen his people and he sticks by them.

• **How do you think that might have helped him to pray?** Nehemiah is putting his mind beyond his circumstance—zooming in on the all-powerful God instead of focusing on his own brokenness. He names the attributes

of God that he is going to need—his power and loyalty to his people—setting up his prayer on the basis of what God is like. This gives him the confidence to pray boldly.

4. What's the contrast between God and the people (v 5, 6-7)? God is loyal to his people, but his people have not been loyal to him! He has kept his covenant with them, but they have not kept their covenant with him. They have repeatedly disobeyed him.

5. What did God say he would do if the people were unfaithful (v 8)? He would scatter them. (This is not an exact quotation but a paraphrase of something God says numerous times—for example in Deuteronomy 4:25-27.) This is exactly the situation Nehemiah is in right now: God has taken his people out of their land and scattered them.

• **But what promise is Nehemiah hoping he will fulfill now (v 9)?** God promised to gather those who turned back to him. Nehemiah is hoping God will bring the people back to Jerusalem and give them his presence again.

6. What has God done for his people that makes this possible (v 9, 10)? God gathers his people and dwells among them (v 9). He redeems them and makes them his people (v 10).

EXPLORE MORE
Read Revelation 21:1-4
What does the new Jerusalem have in common with the old Jerusalem (v 3)? God is said to dwell in both cities.
But what makes it better (v 4)? There will be no mourning, no crying, no dying, and no pain. No deprivation or injustice or crime.

7. APPLY: What do you think it looks like for us to represent God's rule today? Nehemiah's prayer shows us that being faithful to God and keeping his commandments is crucial to representing his rule (v 5, 9). Encourage the group to be practical and specific in how they apply this. We need to worship God, to read his word, and listen to good teaching—and we need to put that teaching into practice. We need to care passionately about God's reputation, putting his power and his character on display in our lives just as it was on display in the physical city of Jerusalem. We need to weep for the broken and cry out in prayer. We need to be active in obeying him, and at the same time recognize our total dependence on him.

- **Where do you see brokenness in the representation of God's rule today? What will you ask him to rebuild?** Think about your own lives, the life of the church, and the life of the communities around you. We should be aiming to see something like the beauty of the new Jerusalem in the world around us (see Explore More above). Wherever there is sin or brokenness, we should be active in rebuilding for God's glory. Again, this is a question that should have some practical answers specific to your context.

8. How does Nehemiah's conversation with the king begin (2:1-2)? The scene is a drinking party. Nehemiah is the cupbearer to the king—basically the king's personal bartender. He's standing there in the middle of the party, but he's visibly sad. Artaxerxes notices this.

9. In verses 4-8, how do we see Nehemiah's dependence on the Lord? Before Nehemiah replies to the king's question, he prays a quick silent prayer (v 4). He needs God's help with what he is about to say. At the end of the passage, he tells us, "The good hand of my God was upon me" (v 8). God is actively involved. Nehemiah knows this.

- **How do we see his own hard work and initiative?** Nehemiah has already made meticulous plans. He knows exactly what he needs from the king. He knows how long his trip will take (v 6). He knows he needs letters from the king to show he's on official business, in case he meets with opposition (v 7). He knows exactly what he wants to build and what he needs to build it (v 8).

10. What does the king grant Nehemiah? He gives Nehemiah everything he has asked for. He will send him to Judah for more than a year (the time it would take to get from Susa to Jerusalem and back). He will give him letters of recommendation. He will tell Asaph to provide timber.

- **Why?** Nehemiah doesn't say that he got what he wanted because he was gifted or because he was persuasive or because he had planned meticulously or even because he had been diligent in prayer. He tells us, "The good hand of my God was upon me" (v 8). It was all the work of God.

11. APPLY: How can we use Nehemiah's example in our own conversations with unbelievers? Take each of the things in the paragraph above and discuss really practically what it could look like for us today. Think about people or groups you are trying to reach: what common ground could you find with them? What could you do to prepare to share the gospel with them? What opportunities to share the good news are you not yet taking?

12. APPLY: What do Nehemiah's actions throughout 1:1 – 2:8 teach us about what it looks like to prepare to represent God's rule to those around us? Nehemiah cares passionately about representing God's rule. He gets into God's presence. He repents of sin. He uses the opportunities he has in his work role. He plans carefully. He keeps on praying. All these things are ways we ourselves can work for God's kingdom.

- **How can we put these things into practice today?** Encourage the group to think really practically about where they could put these things into practice.

Nehemiah 2:9 – 3:32

2 BUILDING A TEAM

THE BIG IDEA
Being on mission for God involves careful leadership and planning, but it also involves people from all walks of life working together in unity.

SUMMARY
Nehemiah has made careful plans already, but as he heads to Jerusalem, we see how his awareness of the situation changes. He has arrived in the province (v 9) and met with hostility from two local leaders, Sanballat and Tobiah. So when he gets to Jerusalem he stays quiet about his plans until he has surveyed the city (v 11-16). He sees his mission as a God-inspired work, and has utter confidence in it; but he knows he needs to test the details of his plan before sharing it.

In verse 17 Nehemiah is ready to call the people together, share his vision, and unify those who are willing to aid God's mission. He starts by saying, "You see the trouble we are in" (v 17)—including himself in the suffering and identifying with them. Nehemiah is a pointer to Jesus here and an example to us as we minister to others.

In order to establish unity among the people, Nehemiah tells them how God has been helping him so far (v 18). As soon as they hear that God is with them, they are ready to join in. Sanballat and Tobiah try to dissuade them by accusing Nehemiah of rebelling against the king, but Nehemiah remains confident that God will make it happen. He is not interested in trying to persuade these opponents to join his mission, but bluntly tells them that they are in the wrong.

In chapter 3 we see how God uses human hands to build. The people have committed themselves in a unity to build, and now they start the work. People from all walks of life are working together on the wall. Despite very different backgrounds, they all prioritize God's plans.

OPTIONAL EXTRA
Play a game which shows the importance of working together in unity. Each person must fold a piece of paper in half horizontally, and in half again. Then open it out again. On the top section, draw the head of a monster. Then fold the paper so that the

top section can't be seen. At the edge of each of the following sections, write three words to describe your monster. (They can be the same words each time, or different ones!) Then pass the paper to the next person. Each person should now draw a torso which they think might match the head, based on the three-word description they can see. Fold the paper back again and pass it along. The next person draws legs, again based on the description. The final person draws feet. Pass the papers along once more, open them up, and see how unified your monsters are!

GUIDANCE FOR QUESTIONS

1. What do you think holds people back from joining in with the ministries or missional work of their church? Some people may feel they just can't—either because they don't have the skills, or because they are in difficult circumstances such as illness. Others tend to think of church as somewhere just to receive. They want to enjoy worshiping God and being part of a church family, but they don't see the need to be active workers for the Lord. Today's study should encourage and equip the first group, and challenge the thinking of the second.

2. Why does Nehemiah's request for letters of recommendation (see v 7-8) prove to be wise (v 10)? He meets with hostility from Sanballat the Horonite and Tobiah the Ammonite. Sanballat is the governor of the region and he doesn't care for the welfare of the Israelites or Jerusalem. But the king's letters mean that these enemies have to let Nehemiah get on with his mission.

3. In verses 11-16, how else does Nehemiah show caution? Nehemiah

doesn't tell anyone what his plans are (v 12, 16) and only takes a few men and one animal with him so as not to cause a stir (v 12).

4. How does he describe his plans (v 12)? Nehemiah calls his vision "what my God had put into my heart to do." He sees it as a God-inspired work.

5. When he does speak to the people, how does Nehemiah describe the problems in Jerusalem (v 17)? He says they are in "trouble," suffering "derision." Jerusalem is in ruins and its gates have been burned.

• **Why do you think he uses the words "we" and "us"?** Nehemiah doesn't separate himself from the circumstances of the people he is ministering to but enters into their issues and includes his lot with them.

6. APPLY: In your church or small group, how could you promote a culture of helping one another and identifying with one another and those around you? We should be relevant—understanding and speaking into the communities we serve. We should own the issues of those we are serving—letting their problems become our problems. Encourage the group to think practically about how to do this in your context.

7. How does Nehemiah encourage the people to get on board with his plans (2:18)? He speaks about the "hand of … God." God has already acted to help Nehemiah—proof that God is concerned about his people's condition. God is with them.

• **How does he describe them (v 20)?**

They are God's servants.

8. Why do you think Nehemiah's words encourage a sense of unity? God's work among them gives them their identity and purpose. They can work together because they are working for him.

9. What's Nehemiah's attitude to those who don't agree with his plans? Nehemiah doesn't argue with his opponents at all. He doesn't take them seriously. He could pull out his letter from the king to prove his innocence or go over the law of the Persian empire, but instead he simply says, *God is going to make it happen, and you're not part of it.* He recognizes them as his opponents rather than trying to persuade them, and is clear and direct.

10. What groups of people do we see working on the wall (3:1, 8, 9, 12)? The priests (v 1); goldsmiths and perfumers (v 8); the son of one of the rulers of Jerusalem (v 9); another of the rulers of Jerusalem, along with his daughters (v 12).

• **Who would be the equivalent groups of people today? Can you imagine them all working together on a building project?** The priests are the spiritual leaders. An equivalent today would be church leaders. The goldsmiths and perfumers are today's bankers and business owners. The rulers of the districts of Jerusalem are the politicians of their day. It's hard to imagine a building project in which the church pastor works beside the business owners who work beside the teenagers who work beside the mayor!

EXPLORE MORE
Read 1 Peter 2:9. What does Peter say is the point of being a royal priesthood? "That you may proclaim the excellencies of

him who called you out of darkness into his marvelous light." In other words, to represent God to those around us and bring them to him.

How can the church take a lead in serving our communities today? It might be through outreach ministries or social enterprises run out of the church itself, or through every individual Christian taking whatever opportunities they have to serve their community. Encourage the group to be practical in sharing ideas about this question.

11. Nehemiah's rebuilding project is all going to plan. Why do you think that is?
• Nehemiah's leadership. He has prepared carefully and shown discretion as he has developed his plans. He has identified closely with the people he is among, being a servant leader rather than a selfish one. He has sought God's will all the way, and trusted him despite opposition.
• The willingness of the people. They commit themselves in a unity to build. People from all walks of life come to be part of God's rebuilding initiative. They choose to come to Jerusalem, a broken-down city, because their priorities are God's priorities.
• The hand of God. Nehemiah is clear that this is God's vision from start to finish (2:12, 20).

12. APPLY: What lessons can be learned from this passage today by...
• **those in leadership?** Like Nehemiah, we should be rooted in relationship with God, so that our vision is his vision. We should be practical and prepared to tweak our plans. We should show carefulness and discretion in our planning. We should own the issues in the communities we seek to serve, aiming to work together with others rather than ordering them around.

- **those who are part of a team running a ministry?** Some of the lessons are the same as those for ministry leaders. We should all be rooted in relationship with God, finding our encouragement and inspiration from him, like the people in 2:18. We should all own the issues in the communities we seek to serve. This passage also calls us to be unified around God's building project, and to be servant-hearted as we work—not thinking of ourselves more than others but joining in humbly with whatever needs to be done, like the rulers of Jerusalem who labor on the wall.

- **those who feel they can't serve, or don't know how?** If you're part of a church, you're part of the community mission of that church. Nehemiah 3 shows us people with very different skill sets and backgrounds coming together on a single project. Likewise, all of us are part of God's rebuilding project. He values us as his servants and fellow-workers. We should encourage one another to take an active part in whatever way we can!

3 Nehemiah 4:1-23
DEVELOPMENT AND DEFENSE

THE BIG IDEA

When opposition strikes, we must be prepared to fight. Ultimately, God is the one who fights for us.

SUMMARY

In Nehemiah 4, Nehemiah and the people of Jerusalem meet with serious opposition. As we watch what happens, we learn how to continue to be productive for God's kingdom in the midst of opposition.

The opposition starts with mockery from Sanballat and Tobiah (v 1-3). They are concerned that the Jews will succeed in rebuilding the city and glorifying God. So they try to discourage them. Nehemiah responds by going straight into a prayer (v 4-5). He is hurt and essentially prays that Sanballat and Tobiah would go to hell. This sounds violent, but notice that Nehemiah doesn't act violently. He vents in prayer and lets God deal with it. He gets on with

building the wall (v 6).

Then the situation intensifies. Opponents from nations in every direction work together to plot against Jerusalem (v 7-8). The Jews respond in prayer and take precautions to make sure they can continue to build (v 9). They focus on God, their help and their strength.

But God's people gradually become weakened in their hearts (v 10-12). They are discouraged and wonder whether it is worth it to continue. Nehemiah finds out and tells everybody to get on the wall. He lines them up with their weapons (v 13). Then he reminds them that they serve the great and awesome God, and calls on them to contend while they build (v 14).

God's enemies' plans are frustrated (v 15). Why? Because the people have stopped walking in fear and started walking in faith again. They are ready to fight. The rest of chapter 4 shows how the people continue to combine defense and development. They understand that God will fight for them (v 20) and this gives them courage to continue to build even when under fire.

OPTIONAL EXTRA
Bring some information about Christians who are being persecuted for their faith, either in your own country or around the world. This will help inform your prayers at the end of the study.

GUIDANCE FOR QUESTIONS
1. What opposition might Christians face today and why? You might talk about the worldwide church and countries in which there is particular persecution. You might talk about opposition from secular culture—whether that's explicit opposition or simply the promotion of ideals and principles that run counter to the Christian worldview. You might talk about opposition within the church itself when people disagree about how things should be run.

2. What do Sanballat and Tobiah say about the rebuilding project (v 2-3)? Sanballat's mocking questions imply that the Jews are feeble, so they won't restore the walls, they won't make a sacrifice, they won't finish in a day, they won't use the heaps of rubbish in Jerusalem to make a strong wall. Tobiah builds on this mockery by saying that the wall is so weak that it won't stand if a fox goes up on it.

• **Why do you think they say these things?** Nehemiah tells us Sanballat is "angry and greatly enraged" (v 1). So he attacks the building project verbally—hoping to discourage those who are part of it.

3. Nehemiah responds by venting in prayer. What does he ask God to do (v 4-5)? He tells God not to forgive these enemies, but to punish them by allowing them to be plundered and taken captive. *Let them all go to hell* is the essence of what he's saying. Nehemiah's prayer shows how seriously he takes God's work. It's right to get angry when God is opposed. Nehemiah's words are extreme—but the point is that he is bringing his anger to God rather than lashing out. The Bible does warn of the destruction of those who oppose God (e.g. 2 Thessalonians 1:5-10; 2 Peter 2), but it is always God who is the judge and the destroyer. He is the only one whose anger is always completely just. So when we're opposed, when we're hurt, we need to bring our anger to him.

• **What action does he take (v 6)?** Nehemiah just gets on with building the wall. He doesn't retaliate against Tobiah and Sanballat.

4. How do you think Nehemiah felt at this point? Nehemiah is hurt. He is sick of these people and their insults! Yet he doesn't let his feelings take him off focus. He ignores the haters and keeps doing what God has called him to do.

• **What about the other builders (v 6)?** They don't shut down in the midst of opposition. They have "a mind to work."

5. How does the opposition intensify (v 7-8)? Nehemiah's opponents go from jeering to plotting. People who don't usually get together start meeting. Sanballat's group, the Samaritans, are from the north; the Arabs are from the south, the Ashdodites from the west, and the Ammonites from the east. Between them they surround Jerusalem—and they're all getting together to fight God's people.

- **How do Nehemiah and the people respond?** With prayer again—and with action. "We prayed to our God and set a guard as a protection against them day and night" (v 9). They take sensible precautions to make sure they can keep going. And they focus on God, their help and their strength.

6. What does all this teach us about how to deal with opposition to God's work today?
- We have to recognize what is really happening. Opposition is about God, not us. Knowing that should free us to respond proportionately rather than feeling personally wounded.
- We have to put our minds on God. "[God] keep[s] him in perfect peace whose mind is stayed on [him]" (Isaiah 26:3). He is bigger than our circumstances. We should go to him in prayer—both to vent, and to ask him to act.
- We have to stay focused. Don't let opposition get in the way of what God told you to do. Asking God to act doesn't mean we don't take action ourselves—we have to keep going with the work he has called us to.

EXPLORE MORE
Read 1 Peter 2:21-23
What did Jesus do to those who threatened and mocked him? He did not threaten or mock in response. His character remained intact. He continued doing what God had called him to do, undeterred.
How do we see Nehemiah doing the same? What does he do as a way of "entrusting himself to him who judges justly"? Nehemiah doesn't respond directly to his mockers but turns straight to God.

7. What further discouragements do the builders face (v 10-12)?
- v 10: They are getting sick and tired of the opposition and they are becoming weakened in their hearts. "By ourselves we will not be able to rebuild the wall," they are saying to one another. They've been paying too much attention to the words of Sanballat and his cronies!
- v 11: Their enemies are turning up the heat with fresh threats.
- v 12: Other Jews who live nearby but aren't part of the building project come and try to dissuade them from carrying on.

8. How does Nehemiah encourage them (v 14)? He doesn't simply tell them to muster up courage. First, he tells them, *I want you to look at who God is.* "Remember the Lord, who is great and awesome." This is the God who dwells in unapproachable light (1 Timothy 6:16)—and who fights for his people. He is on their side. Second, he reminds them who they are fighting for. They're not just saving their own skins. They're fighting for others.

- **What's the result (v 15)?** The enemy's plan of scaring the people into giving up won't work. Why? Because the people have stopped walking in fear and started walking in faith again.

9. What is Nehemiah's new strategy for making sure the building continues?
- **v 16** Some build, while others stand ready with weapons.
- **v 17-18** The builders strap swords to their sides so that they are ready to fight even while they build.
- **v 19-20** A trumpeter is ready to blow a ram's horn and call everyone together into one place, to receive instructions and go into battle.

- **v 21** They work from dawn til dusk.
- **v 22-23** They stay in the city overnight to guard the work. Nehemiah and his closest companions are constantly ready to fight, even at night.

10. The trumpet will call them all together to fight—but what's an even better thing to rally around (v 20)? God! The people understand that God is the one who fights for them. He is the one who makes them strong.

11. In what ways does God fight for us…
- **in the person of Jesus (see Colossians 2:15; Romans 8:34)?** On the cross, Jesus disarmed evil (Colossians 2:15). So he has already won the victory for us. Now he intercedes for us at the Father's right hand (Romans 8:34): his prayers are for us.
- **in the person of the Holy Spirit (see Ephesians 1:13-14; 6:17; Galatians 5:22-23)?** The Spirit continues to develop and rebuild us. He guarantees our salvation (Ephesians 1:13-14). He keeps us safe against the evil one (Ephesians 6:17). He develops and rebuilds us (Galatians 5:22-23).

12. APPLY: Nehemiah calls the people to fight for their brothers (i.e., their fellow Jews), their sons and daughters, and their wives (v 14). What will it look like for us to do this today—fighting for God's glory in our lives and others'?
- We should be contending for our spiritual brothers and sisters: praying and standing up for those who are our brothers and sisters in Christ in other countries and other communities.
- We should also fight for those who are members of our community in a non-spiritual sense. As those who believe in the God who hates sin and promises restoration, we should be concerned about the people who are worst off in our countries and in our neighborhoods. That means seeking to share the gospel, most importantly; but also caring for people socially and doing good deeds for those who need them.
- Fighting for our children means fighting to ensure that they can't remember a day when Jesus wasn't being invested into their souls. It could mean developing a family worship time in which we point them heavenward; teaching them the Bible; and talking to them about what it means to follow Christ.
- Fighting for our wives (or husbands!) means fighting to keep our marriages going when things are hard. It means seeking God together and building one another up in faith.

4 Nehemiah 5:1-19
WALKING IN THE FEAR OF GOD

THE BIG IDEA
The fear of God means standing up for justice, showing grace and mercy, and surrendering our rights to serve others.

SUMMARY
Jerusalem is now facing an economic crisis. The landless are short of food (v 2) and the landowners are compelled to mortgage their properties (v 3). Some are forced to borrow money at exorbitant rates because of oppressive taxation (v 4), and some even have to sell their children into slavery to pay off their debts (v 5).

But Nehemiah hears the people's cries and brings legal charges against the officials and well-to-do people who have been oppressing the poor (v 6-8). He calls them to "walk in the fear of our God"—repenting of their unjust actions and repairing the damage they have done by returning the property and money they have taken unfairly (v 9-11). Nehemiah is modeling something of what Jesus would come to bring: as well as guaranteeing justice and reparation for the poor, he gives the oppressors a chance to repent and change their ways. But he also gives them an ultimatum. If they go back to their sinful ways, they will run out of chances (v 13). They have to take their sin seriously.

In verses 14-19 we learn that Nehemiah has taken upon himself the expense and pain of looking after the people in the city of Jerusalem. In a way, the punishment for the injustice has been laid on him,

because he has made sacrifices for them. As governor of Judah, he has the right to add his own tax onto the king's taxes, in order to pay his salary and his employees' salary and buy their food (v 14-15). Previous governors had abused that right, but Nehemiah is concerned for the welfare of the people. So he foregoes his right altogether, and sends his servants out to work on the wall instead of serving him, and pays for huge quantities of food at his own expense (v 16-18). He is bending over backward to serve the people, for the glory of God. He is an example to us!

OPTIONAL EXTRA
Research some local charities or ministries beforehand and bring some information about them. Use this to discuss what you could do practically to promote justice and help people in your local community.

GUIDANCE FOR QUESTIONS
1. What are some causes of injustice we see in the world today? You might discuss large-scale issues like economic inequality; corruption and abuse of power; racism; and climate issues. You could also discuss the heart issues that lead to these injustices, such as greed, selfishness, and ignorance.

2. What must people do to get food (v 3)? They are mortgaging their fields, vineyards, and houses. This was not normal in Nehemiah's time as it might be today. It is putting them in a very vulnerable position.

• **What else are they being forced to do**

(v 4, 5)? They have to pay taxes, which means even more borrowing of money. So now they're in debt. In this culture when you couldn't pay your bills you used your possessions as collateral. But they also used children. They put their children into slavery, to serve without wages until the debt had been repaid. And this is what the people in Jerusalem do.

3. How does Nehemiah feel when he hears about this (v 6)? He is very angry!

• What two charges does he bring against the nobles and officials (v 7, 8)? First, they are exacting interest on their loans. This was against Jewish law (Deuteronomy 23:19). Second, they are forcing into slavery the very people whose freedom Nehemiah has bought from foreign masters.

4. Nehemiah sums up what they are doing as not walking in the fear of God (v 9). Why do you think "fear of God" is at the root of acting justly? Walking in the fear of God means taking God seriously. And God is a just God. He does right always. It is because God is just that we can know what justice is and act with justice ourselves. If we know God, if we are awestruck by him, it should make us reach out to help others and never to exploit them.

5. What is Nehemiah's solution (v 10-11)? He tells the nobles to repent. They ought to return everything they have been given as collateral for debt, including all the interests they have been paid. In other words, all the people's debts are to be cleared.

EXPLORE MORE
Read Luke 4:16-21
What is Jesus' mission statement? To proclaim good news to the poor, liberty to the captives, and recovery of sight to the blind, to set at liberty those who are oppressed, and to proclaim the year of the Lord's favor.

How did Nehemiah put this into practice? Nehemiah freed the oppressed from their debts and released those who had been sold into slavery.

How did Jesus put this into practice? In his earthly life Jesus did bring good news, give sight to the blind, and proclaim the year of the Lord's favor. But the favor Jesus came to proclaim is not primarily economic and physical freedom. He came not only to free particular individuals but most importantly to put an end to injustice forever. The favor Jesus came to proclaim is about gaining forgiveness for sin, transformation inside out, and life for eternity. All this he achieved on the cross.

6. How does he urge them to take this second chance seriously (v 13)? Nehemiah gives them an ultimatum. He prays that God will "shake out every man from his house and from his labor who does not keep this promise." They have a second chance, but ultimately, if they go back to their sinful ways, they will run out of chances. They need to take their sins seriously.

7. APPLY: What unjust situations do you see around you today? Encourage the group to think about this question on a very local level—small injustices they see at work or in their families—then on the level of the communities they live in, and finally on a national and a global scale.

• What will it look like to respond as Nehemiah did? We must listen to people's cries (v 1). We must seek truth, justice, and the reparation of wrongs (v 7-11). We must invite repentance (v 10-11) and show mercy while being clear about the seriousness of sin (v 13). Encourage the group to be practical as they think about how to apply these things to the situations you have discussed.

8. What right does Nehemiah have as governor (v 14-15)? He had the right to add his own tax onto the king's taxes in order to pay his salary and his employees' salaries and to buy their food.

• **Previous governors have abused that right (v 15), but Nehemiah decides not to use it at all. Why not (v 15, 18)?** Nehemiah fears God (v 15) and wishes not to put too heavy a burden on the people, who can't afford to pay this tax (v 18).

9. What do he and his servants do instead of growing food (v 16)? They work on the wall.

10. Nehemiah is not just paying for his own food—what does he pay for and who does this serve (v 17-18)? Every single day the cooks prepared one entire ox, six of the best sheep, and six birds. Every week that's 7 cows, 42 sheep, and 42 birds, not to mention the wine! This was to provide for 150 people, including the "Jews and officials" who were helping him to run the province and rebuild the city, as well as people from other nations. These were not God's people, but they would come close and see the beauty of God in the life of the people of God at Nehemiah's table. He was serving them into the kingdom.

11. APPLY: Western culture has a philosophy of entitlement: we often talk about our rights or about what we deserve. How does this passage challenge that? Nehemiah surrenders his rights. This is because he believes that what

God wants to do is more important than his personal preferences and desires. Instead of focusing on what he is entitled to, he thinks about what opportunities he has to serve others for the sake of God. We should do the same.

• **What situations can you think of today where giving up our rights would be a way of serving others?** Answers could include giving away money; giving up our right to intimacy in marriage for a period; giving up our preferences about how church is run; giving up time we have set aside for ourselves, when others need help; and many other things!

12. APPLY: Nehemiah exemplifies Micah 6:8: "What does the LORD require of you but to do justice, and to love kindness, and to walk humbly with your God?" Why do you think these things express "the fear of God"—the lordship of God in our lives? We "do justice" because we have a God of justice. We want to do what pleases him and we take his judgment seriously. We "love kindness" because we have a God who is kind and merciful— giving sinners a second chance and being generous to those who deserve his wrath. We recognize his kindness to us and this motivates us to be kind to others. We walk humbly with God—recognizing his lordship and putting his priorities first—because we know that we are tiny, insignificant, and foolish next to him.

• **How can we put each of these things into practice?** We can "do justice" by intervening where we see oppression, poverty, violence, and debt; and by upholding justice in our own dealings. We can "love kindness" by being generous with what we have, laying down our rights, and serving those around us in any way we can. We "walk humbly with [our] God" by seeking him in prayer and asking

him to act to transform situations—and to transform us.

5 Nehemiah 6:1 – 7:4
STAY FOCUSED

THE BIG IDEA
We need to stay focused on God and his mission. We need clarity of purpose. This is what will enable us to be effective kingdom workers.

SUMMARY
In Nehemiah 6, the building of the wall is almost complete (v 1). What happens next is that the enemy turns up the heat. Sanballat and Geshem are no longer trying to attack the work as a whole. Instead they are trying to take out Nehemiah. They try to persuade him to come out and meet them (v 2). But Nehemiah, realizing that they want to do him harm, says no (v 3-4). He remains focused on the work. He knows it won't get done without him there.

Next Sanballat sends a letter full of slander against Nehemiah—an open letter which anyone can read (v 5-7). Once again it's clear what these enemies are trying to do: they want to stop the work on the wall (v 9). Nehemiah knows that the battle is not his, but the Lord's. So he doesn't waste words or energy getting upset or defending himself at length. He simply says, *You're lying* (v 8), and prays to God for strength (v 9).

Next, it's one of Nehemiah's own people who tries to take him off focus (v 10-11). Shemaiah claims to have a warning from God and invites Nehemiah to take refuge in

the temple. But Nehemiah knows that God has not sent Shemaiah: he's been hired by Sanballat and Tobiah (v 12-13). It would be a sin for Nehemiah to go into the temple, so he refuses to go in. He knows what the plan of the Lord is and he trusts it.

Once again, Nehemiah chooses not to retaliate or to try to deal with his enemies in his own strength. He offers up a prayer instead (v 14), asking God to fight for him.

"So the wall was finished" (v 15)—and quickly. It is noticeable that God has been with them. Because of this, people in the surrounding nations are afraid (v 16). They are realizing that God, whose work they are opposing, is in control.

However, the completion of the wall does not put an end to hostility—and again the opposition comes from within. Certain nobles send letters to Tobiah, the enemy of God, telling him what's happening in Jerusalem (v 17). These families have bound themselves with promises to Tobiah and linked themselves with him by marriage (v 18). They also try to persuade Nehemiah that Tobiah is a good man. Once again, however, Nehemiah knows Tobiah's true motivation: "to make me afraid" (v 19).

In the first few verses of chapter 7, we see Nehemiah taking action to protect the work that has been done so far and allow for future development in the city. He appoints officials in the temple (v 1), trustworthy leaders for the city (v 2), and guards for the gates (v 3). He does everything he can to maintain focus on God's work.

OPTIONAL EXTRA
Hold a staring competition. Who can focus for the longest time?

GUIDANCE FOR QUESTIONS
1. "Focus matters. You can have all the abilities and opportunities in the world, but if you don't have focus, you'll never get anywhere." Do you agree? In what situations might this be true? Encourage the group to think about what focus really means and when it is useful. Answers could vary from sporting scenarios to educational settings to busy periods at work or many other things.

2. What do Sanballat, Tobiah, and Geshem do first of all to try to take Nehemiah off focus (v 2-4)? They want him to leave the work and the city and come out to meet them. So they write to suggest a meeting—five times!

3. Why might Nehemiah be tempted to do what they want? It seems like a friendly invitation. Maybe they will be able to negotiate an agreement and an end to hostility.

- **Why doesn't he?** Nehemiah realizes what is really going on: they intend to do him harm (v 2). Yet his own safety is not his chief concern. When he sends messages back to say he won't come, the message is, "I am doing a great work and I cannot come down" (v 3). He remains focused on the task God has given him to do.

4. What is God's enemies' next tactic (v 4-7)? Now Sanballat is accusing him of rebelling against King Artaxerxes and setting himself up as a king. He sends this slander in an open letter—which means anyone could read it on the way to Nehemiah. Sanballat wants as many people as possible to read his accusations.

5. How would you have responded if you were Nehemiah? You might be tempted to make a proclamation to counter the slander. Or to write to the king to assure him of your loyalty. Or to send soldiers against Sanballat to limit any further damage. But Nehemiah does none of these things.

- **How does he actually respond (v 8)?** He is completely straightforward: *You're lying!* He doesn't waste words or energy getting upset or defending himself at length.

EXPLORE MORE
Read Colossians 3:3, 9-10. What makes it possible to "seek the things that are above"? In Christ we have died to sin (v 3, 9) and been given a new self (v 10). God is renewing us day by day to be like him.
Read Colossians 3:12-17. What do these verses tell us about what it means to "seek the things that are above"? We should be compassionate, kind, humble, meek, patient, forgiving, and full of love. We should let the peace of Christ rule in our hearts, be thankful, be saturated with the word of Christ, teach and admonish one another, and sing praises to God—and all in the name of the Lord Jesus.

6. APPLY: What things today might seem reasonable or attractive but would stop us focusing on God or his mission? You might be attracted to a person romantically. But if he or she will not lead you toward Christ but away from him, it's a come-down. You might be offered a promotion. But the new job might take you away from serving in God's mission. It might seem reasonable to skip church for a one-off event like a match or family visit, but you end up skipping more and more. It might seem sensible to save lots of money, but that can lead to a lack of generosity toward God and his people. It can be tempting to allow kids' education and extra-curricular activities to take priority over our (and their) spiritual lives and church commitment. Add your own examples!

- **What negative or difficult things might take us off focus?** Suffering often tempts us to stop focusing on God. It could be physical illness, depression, or bereavement. Or it could be opposition or broken relationships. Encourage the group to think what Sanballat might be saying or doing if he were in their lives!

7. Shemaiah claims to have a prophecy from the Lord for Nehemiah. But where does it really come from (6:10-13)? Tobiah and Sanballat. Their plan is to pay this man to scare Nehemiah and persuade him to fall into sin by entering the temple.

- **How does Nehemiah know it cannot come from God?** It contradicts God's law. Nehemiah knows that it is a sin for him to go into the temple (v 13). Only priests and temple attendants can go inside the actual temple building (2 Chronicles 23:6). So God can't be telling Nehemiah to go in.

8. How do you think Nehemiah's prayer in verse 14 helps him to stay focused on the task at hand? He is choosing not to retaliate or to try to deal with his enemies in his own strength. He knows that God can fight better than he can himself. He knows

that one day God will call them to account, and so he can concentrate on the work in the meantime.

9. How do people in the surrounding nations respond to the completion of the walls (v 16)? They are afraid and fall greatly in their own esteem.

- **Why do you think their understanding of what has happened leads to this response?** They are realizing that God, whose work they are opposing, is more powerful than they knew. In fact, he is sovereign: in control of everything, seen and unseen. They realize that they are far smaller and less powerful than him.

10. What has taken the nobles of Judah off focus (v 18-19)? They are "bound by oath" to Tobiah (v 18). Not only are they related to him by marriage but they have also promised to support him. They are more concerned about their own personal benefits and alliances than God's kingdom.

- **What do they do as a result (v 17, 19)?** They send letters to Tobias to inform him about what's happening in Jerusalem, and they try to persuade Nehemiah that Tobiah is a good man.

11. What two things does Nehemiah do to maintain focus after the walls are finished (7:2, 3)? He chooses faithful and God-fearing men to be in charge of the city—not the corrupt nobles but people he can trust to look out for God's interests. He tells them to put guards around the city to protect the work they have done so far and enable the city inside the walls to be developed.

12. APPLY: What can we learn from Nehemiah about how to remain focused

on God and his mission? How can you put these things into practice?

- Prayer. Nehemiah asks God for help. He is constantly open to God, often praying brief prayers as he goes along. We too can cultivate the habit of praying short prayers whenever we need strength or help.
- Trust. Nehemiah recognizes that it is God's work he is doing. That means he prioritizes God's work above anything else. It also means he is not afraid of his enemies but trusts God to look after him. If we trust in God, we will prioritize his work above all things. This will keep us from fear and from distraction.
- Knowledge of Scripture. Nehemiah knows God's law and can recognize when someone is trying to get him to disobey it. Likewise, the Bible keeps us focused. When we hear advice from people, our first question should be: what does the Bible say?
- Building a team. Nehemiah appoints God-fearing people to be in charge of the city. It's people like that we need to have around us. We should not just seek buddies but faithful and God-fearing people.

6 Nehemiah 7:5 – 8:18
REBUILT THROUGH THE WORD

THE BIG IDEA
The Bible is God's word, which shows us how to live. We should treat it with reverence and allow our communities to be shaped by it.

SUMMARY
In chapter 7, Nehemiah takes an inventory of all God's people. He is getting ready to assemble everyone together (v 5). We're seeing community formation: Nehemiah wants to know who is a member and who's just an attender. Who is actually ready to represent God's reign?

In chapter 8 this newly defined community is ready to assemble all together in one place, to listen to the Scriptures. Ezra, a priest and one of the key leaders of the people at this time, brings the Law—the first five books of today's Old Testament—and everyone listens to it being read (8:1-4). Their reverence for God's word is clear: they listen from daybreak to midday (v 3), stand when the book is opened (v 5), and worship God by lifting their hands, bowing their heads, and even laying their faces to the ground, as Ezra begins to read (v 6).

In verses 7-8 God's word is read again. This time, experts in the Law disperse all through the congregation and explain some of the words so that the people can understand the reading. They hold their small-group meetings right there in their church service! The point is that when the people understand the word, then they can live it out.

Now the people's tears of joy turn into tears of conviction (v 9). They recognize that there is a distance between the way they are living and the way the word of God calls them to live. But the leaders say, *No!* God wants us to be convicted of our sin, but he doesn't want us to stay in our sin. Nehemiah and the other leaders want to celebrate the fact that God is giving his people a new start. The people are to celebrate what God is doing among them (v 9-12).

On the second day, the leaders gather for a little seminary class just by themselves (v 13). They find the instructions for the Feast of Booths or Tabernacles, in Leviticus 23. This festival pointed back to the days when Israel experienced God's faithfulness in the wilderness. It was a reminder of all the sin and grumbling that God put up with over that time, and how gracious God was to them even then. The leaders now put out a decree calling everyone to put these instructions into action (v 14-15). Everyone gathers leafy branches and makes booths to remember the way God dwelt with his people in the wilderness (v 17).

These people are fresh out of captivity. They have seen Jerusalem half destroyed and built it up again. They have realized that the Scriptures haven't really been taught and put into practice by them as a nation for decades. Now they are ready to celebrate God's faithfulness properly again. They read the Law every day—and rejoice in it (v 17-18).

OPTIONAL EXTRA

Use different materials to make model buildings. Divide the group into teams and give each team a different "building material." One of these materials should be well-suited for the task—perhaps children's building blocks or pieces of cardboard—but the others should be more difficult. Try cotton wool or playing cards, for example. Each group should be able to make some

kind of structure, but some will be in much better shape than others! The point is that it matters what we use to build and form ourselves and our communities.

GUIDANCE FOR QUESTIONS

1. How do you find reading God's word? What do you like about it? What is hard? Encourage the group to be honest! This question tees up the subject of the study.

2. Who comes together and why (v 1-2)? "All the people" (v 1)—specifically, "men and women and all who could understand what they heard" (v 2). So this includes teenagers and kids too.

3. How long do they listen for (v 3)? From daybreak to midday. That's about five hours!

4. What measures are taken to make sure people can clearly hear and understand (v 4, 7-8)? They build a wooden platform so that Ezra can be seen as he reads the Scriptures. (This would also help them to see the word of God as exalted—literally higher than them, to remind them to hold it in high regard.) Then the Levites—religious leaders—disperse all through the congregation and explain some of the words so that the people can understand the reading. They hold their small-group meetings right there in the church service!

5. How do they respond to what they hear (v 5-6)? They say "Amen" to Ezra's prayer, lifting up their hands. They stand respectfully as Ezra starts to read. Then they bow to the ground and worship God. They reverence God and his word.

6. APPLY: Do you think Christians today share this reverence for God's word? Why, or why not? The people in Nehemiah are encountering God's word for the first time—or at least the first time in a long time. So they have a sense of wonder and worship which might be hard for us to capture today. This gathering of all the people is a national event of great seriousness, which may feel very different from our church services. There may be other reasons, too, why we don't have this sense of reverence. Do we forget that it is God's word we are hearing? Or are we so familiar with certain passages that we find it hard to really pay attention to them? Perhaps we find God's word hard to understand or it feels too far removed from our daily lives. On the other hand, hopefully in your church the Bible does have a central place. There is probably a recognition that it is at the center of what we do as Christians.

7. APPLY: What could be some ways of showing a right attitude toward God's word as we gather as Christians?
Here are a few ideas:
- Preparing for a Bible study or church service by reading the passage in advance.
- Paying close attention to the sermon— perhaps taking notes.
- Reflecting on what we have heard after the service finishes, either in conversation with others or on our own at home.
- Trying to put into practice what we have learned.
- In Bible studies, really working hard to understand what is going on and what God wants to say to us. Not being afraid to ask questions.
- **What about in our personal reading of the Bible?**
  - Setting aside a regular time to read it.
  - Responding in worship and prayer to

what we have read.
- Taking advantage of notes or commentaries to help us understand what we are reading.
- Some find it helpful to have a particular physical posture as they read or pray, to encourage themselves to have an inward posture of worship and reverence.

8. Why do you think the people respond the way they do as they hear the law (v 9)? They weep because they have recognized that there is a distance between the way they are living and the way the word of God calls them to live.

- **But what are they told to do (v 9-12)?** They should be glad instead of weeping. They should celebrate with feasting and wine, and share with those who don't have their own food and drink ready.

9. Who comes back for more the following day (v 13)? The leaders of the people: the heads of each family, the priests, and the Levites.

10. Why do they build leafy booths (v 14-17)? They are obeying what they have read in God's Law. This is a celebration of the Feast of Booths.

- **Why do you think they rejoice so much at this (v 17)?** This is a moment of community formation and revival. They are going back to what God said they should do and becoming the people they are supposed to be. They are celebrating together. Specifically, they are celebrating their history and God's faithfulness to them—see Explore More for more details on what this festival celebrated.

EXPLORE MORE
Read Leviticus 23:42-43. What are the

people supposed to remember? They are supposed to think of God's faithfulness in bringing his people out of Egypt. **What particular significance do you think this would have had for the people in Nehemiah's time?** The people are fresh out of captivity, much like those in the time of the exodus. For them too, this is a moment of new birth—a time of committing themselves to God and recognizing his faithfulness to them.

11. Why do you think the people are so desperate to saturate themselves in God's word? They recognize that wholeness comes through God's word. The Scriptures are what God uses for "teaching, for reproof, for correction, and for training in righteousness" (2 Timothy 3:16). They are what the people need in order to obey God and live as they should as his people. Encourage the group to really put themselves in the people's shoes here and imagine how they felt and why.

12. APPLY: What can we do to maintain habits of paying attention to God's word, and then putting it into practice? How can we help each other with this? This is a practical question and you should encourage group members to come up with concrete ideas. Here are a few possibilities:
- An accountability relationship whereby you check in with each other about whether you have read a portion of Scripture each day, or ask each other what key thing you have learned.
- Reading Scripture together with another person—either literally meeting up to read together, or reading the same portion of Scripture as one another and texting one another to share thoughts, questions, or application ideas.
- Making a point of discussing the sermon after church on a Sunday.
- Taking notes on what you read in the Bible or hear in sermons.
- Memorizing Bible verses or passages.
- Praying based on what you have read, in order to drive it home to your heart.

7 Nehemiah 9:1 – 12:43
SACRIFICIAL COMMITMENT

THE BIG IDEA
People are faithless but God is faithful. That's our motivation to commit ourselves—and everything we have—to him.

SUMMARY
After the celebration of Nehemiah 8, the people assemble again—but this time they are grieving. Chapter 9 contains an overview of the redemptive record of God in the lives of his people. We see some beautiful things about who God is and what he's done—how he's always been intervening and helping his people. So why do the people grieve? Because before you can appreciate who God is, you have to know who you're not. This is a moment of collective repentance.

They start off with a posture of humility, demonstrated through fasting, wearing sackcloth, and putting dirt on their heads (v 1). They are ready to confess their sins and the sins of their ancestors—so they separate themselves from foreigners, who would have different sins to confess (v 2). Then they spend a quarter of the day reading the Law and another quarter of it confessing and worshiping God (v 3).

The Levites lead the people in a prayer (v 5-38). They speak about the history of God's people, recounting the disobedience and rebellion of their forefathers, and the goodness of God, who was consistently faithful despite the people's faithlessness. They acknowledge that when God has punished his people, he has done that justly. Then they state the difficulties they are in as a result of this pattern of the people's sin and God's discipline (v 36-37). Finally, they rededicate themselves. It is not enough to confess their sin; they want to turn from it and walk in God's ways again. They announce that they are going to make a firm covenant, a binding agreement with God (v 38).

Chapter 10 reveals the terms of this covenant. After a list of the people who signed the document (v 1-27), we are given the text of the agreement (v 28-39). Together, the people promise to observe all God's laws, including not giving their children to foreigners (i.e., those who have not committed themselves to God) in marriage (v 30); keeping the Sabbath day holy (v 31); giving money to pay for the running of the temple (v 32-34); bringing regular offerings as laid out in the Law (v 35-37); and giving tithes (ten percent of income) to pay for the salaries of the Levites, who work in the temple (v 38-39).

Now that the people have committed themselves to the Lord, they have to get themselves organized. 11:1 – 12:26 is a list of who lived where in Jerusalem and the surrounding area, and who played what role.

Once all this has been put in order, they are at last ready to celebrate the finished wall. It's a huge party (12:27-43). Everyone is there. Two choirs parade around the walls, meeting in the temple. Verse 43 sums up the feeling as the grand processions come to their fulfilment: joy. This joy is heard far away. At last, Jerusalem is doing what it is supposed to do: representing God's reign to the people around it.

OPTIONAL EXTRA

Write some joke wedding vows. Give each person an unlikely pair of fictional characters, and tell them to write some imaginary vows for their wedding. What kind of thing would they think it important to promise? Some example pairings: Miss Piggy and Mickey Mouse; Mulan and Huckleberry Finn; Princess Leia and Tarzan; Mary Poppins and Aladdin's genie; Rapunzel and Bilbo Baggins. Or tell the group to choose their own pairings!

GUIDANCE FOR QUESTIONS

1. Why do couples make promises to one another when they get married?
It's an expression of love and mutual trust. Committing themselves to one another out loud in front of all their friends and family will also motivate them to keep their vows! It's a moment they can always look back to, even when things get rocky.

2. In the following verses, what do the Levites say about what God is like and what he's done?
• **v 6** God is unique—the "Lᴏʀᴅ ... alone." He also has a unique level of power. He made the heavens and everything in the

world, and preserves them.

• **v 7-8** God chose Abraham, named him, and made a covenant with him. He is righteous and keeps his promises.

• **v 9-15** God rescued his people out of Egypt. He faithfully protected them as they fled through the Red Sea, faithfully guided them through the wilderness, and provided for them both spiritually (with laws and commandments) and physically (with food and water).

• **v 17-21** God is gracious and merciful, slow to anger and abounding in steadfast love. He did not forsake his people, but continued to guide them, instruct them, and provide for them physically. He bore with them despite their unfaithfulness.

• **v 22-25** God fulfilled his promises to Abraham by bringing his descendants into the promised land. He gave them good land to live in and many children.

3. What about the people? What were they like and what did they do (v 16-18)? They were stiff-necked and disobedient, trying to go back to Egypt instead of proceeding to the promised land. They made a golden calf and worshiped it in God's place. Essentially, they took God for granted and became unfaithful to him.

4. What happened next, repeatedly (v 26, 27, 28, 29-30)? The people rebelled against God and experienced his punishment for their violation of their commitment to him. Yet, as promised, whenever they repented and turned back to the Lord, he responded in mercy and provided deliverance. However, once their people had experienced relief, they returned to their folly. And the cycle continued.

• **What was the culmination of this**

(v 30)? Eventually God sent the people into exile—giving them "into the hand of the peoples of the lands."

5. What situation are the people in now (v 36-37)? They state their difficulties clearly. They have no king or real government of their own but are subject to Artaxerxes. They labor in the fields, but its produce goes to him. Even their bodies are owned by the Persians. (This is possibly a reference to the fact that the Persian rulers drafted their subjects into military service—so the Jews are just cannon fodder.) No wonder that they conclude, "We are in great distress."

• **What do they say about the situation God has put them in (v 33)? Do you agree with their judgment?** They acknowledge that God is innocent and right in his judgments and discipline toward them. In the very consequences for their sins, the Levites see the loyal love of God and his patience toward them throughout every generation.

6. How do they conclude their prayer (v 38)? They make a firm covenant in writing.

• **A covenant is an agreement to be faithful to God. Why do you think it was so important to recount all that history before they get to making this covenant?** They have to be honest about their own sin and their history of unfaithfulness before they can recommit themselves to faithfulness. They have to face the reality of their sin before they can turn from it. They also have to face the reality of their sin in order to admit that they are a mess and to ask for God's help. However, it is not just confessing sin that is happening here. They are also recognizing the faithfulness of God. Again and again, he was faithful to his faithless people. That means there is hope of redemption for Nehemiah's generation, too. The more they focus on the massiveness of who God is, the more they actually forget about the inadequacy of who they are. It all becomes about him. This is what ultimately leads them to commit themselves to him again.

7. APPLY: What strikes you the most about this record of God's dealings with his people? What will you say to him or what will you do as a result? Encourage the group to reflect on the passage and to marvel at the character of God they see here. Hopefully our response should be to commit ourselves to him, just as the people in Nehemiah's time did.

EXPLORE MORE
Read Galatians 3:10-14
Under the Old Testament law, who is cursed (v 10-11)? Everyone! If you rely on the law, you will find that you cannot keep it perfectly, and so you will be cursed. "No one is justified before God by the law."
But how does Jesus change this (v 13)? Jesus cancels out the curses. He has been cursed for our mistakes. Now we gain blessing (v 14).

8. What do they promise to do (v 29)? They promise to keep God's Law.

9. In the promises in the following verses, what sacrifice are the people making, and/or what are they trusting God about?
- **v 30** They're trusting God with their children: they won't give their children in marriage just to anyone, because they want to make sure that they know God and love him. They're sacrificing possible alliances with other families, and trusting

God for their children's future.
- **v 31** They will obey the Sabbath laws. This means making financial sacrifices: they will not work on certain days and therefore they will not earn anything on those days. This is an expression of trust in God's provision.
- **v 32-34** This is another financial commitment. They will give a third of a shekel yearly to the temple. This includes sin offerings to make atonement for Israel. In other words, they are trusting God to forgive them and to allow them to be in relationship with him.
- **v 35-37** They obligate themselves to bring the firstfruits of their crops to the temple, their firstborn animals, the first of their wine and oil, and even their firstborn sons to the Lord. (The sons would be dedicated to God but not left in the temple like the other things!) Notice the repetition of "first." It means that they don't start off by thinking about what they want or need, and then give the leftovers to God. It means that they give the best to God.
- **v 37-39** They also promise tithes. This means ten percent of income, to pay the salaries of the Levites, priests, singers, and other temple servants. They are giving away their money, trusting in God's system of temple sacrifices, and providing for him to be worshiped as he deserves.

10. APPLY: Because of Jesus, we don't have to make sacrifices to pay for our sin. But what does making sacrifices (whether of money, time, or something else) demonstrate about our attitude toward God? In this passage in Nehemiah we see the people making sacrifices simply because they love God and are committed to him. They want to obey his Law because they know it is good—even when that means difficulties along the way. Likewise, we might make sacrifices of money, time, or other things because we are prioritizing God and his ways.

11. APPLY: How can we express commitment to and trust in God when it comes to...
• **our families?** We should be passionate about teaching our children to know and love God. This means leading them in worship, prayer, Bible reading, and practical service. It means giving them good advice about their future and encouraging them to put God first— even if that means we have to be nosy about who they want to date! Trusting in God for our families might also mean trusting him in the pain of infertility or unwanted singleness. It might mean continuing to witness to unbelieving parents, even when they seem unlikely to respond. It might mean working hard to build relationships with those whom God

has made our family in Christ.
• **our finances and work life?** We can express trust in God by resting and not trying to be productive all of the time. We can express commitment to God by giving money to the work of the church and to those who need it.

• **any other area of life?** This is an opportunity to throw the question open more widely. What commitments do people in your group feel called to make? If the group needs some help with any of these questions, encourage them to look at Hebrews 11:6; Matthew 6:25-34; Romans 14:23. These passages may help kick-start your discussion.

12. In verse 43, what do they do to complete the dedication? They make "great sacrifices"—again attesting to their devotion to God.
• **What's the overall feeling here?** Joy! The word is used five times in one verse.

8 Nehemiah 12:44 – 13:31
UNCOMPROMISED FAITH

THE BIG IDEA
Compromising on our obedience is all too easy. We need to watch out and get our lives in order for God.

SUMMARY
In 12:44 – 13:3 we find out two more things that happened on the day when the wall was dedicated. First, things get organized (12:44-47). Officials are appointed to oversee the giving of tithes and contributions which

the people promised back in 10:32-39. The worship in the temple is now fully set up. Second, the people read from the Scriptures again, and they're rocked by what the Lord has said: Ammonites and Moabites are not allowed to be part of the assembly of God (13:1-3). So they separate those of foreign descent. This should not be viewed as racial exclusivity; it's about who is and is not fully committed to God.

But before all this happened, we are told, something else took place which threatened the people's worship and commitment (v 4-5). A priest named Eliashib had been appointed to govern the storerooms in the temple. But he had cleared out one of the rooms and given it to Tobiah—one of God's enemies—as an apartment. When Nehemiah finds out, he gets holy-indignant (v 6-9). He is enraged at this disruption of God's order. He throws Tobiah out, has the chamber cleansed, and restores it to its proper purpose.

This is not the only problem Nehemiah encounters, however. In fact, the people have compromised on all the commitments that they made in chapter 10. First comes the promise of tithes to support the work in the temple (v 10-14): these haven't been given, and so the temple workers have gone elsewhere. Nehemiah sorts this out, appointing new, reliable treasurers to oversee the tithes and temple salaries in the future. Second is the promise to keep the Sabbath (v 15-22). Nehemiah issues orders to prevent any trade from taking place on the Sabbath, and even threatens some of the merchants with physical violence unless they stay away. Third is the promise not to marry foreign wives (v 23-27). This gets Nehemiah even angrier. He uses the example of Solomon to warn the men who have foreign wives about the dangers of allowing their devotion to be compromised. Finally, Nehemiah chases away one last enemy (v 28) and acts again to cleanse the people of God and to establish the work of the temple (v 30-31).

Nehemiah is getting angry for the people's sake, not for his own sake. He doesn't want them to incur God's anger (v 18) or act treacherously against him (v 27). Throughout, the only person

Nehemiah wants to please is God. He is uncompromising in his determination to lead his people to walk in God's ways.

OPTIONAL EXTRA
Play a game of Jenga. When the structure of the tower is compromised, the whole thing falls down!

GUIDANCE FOR QUESTIONS
1. When is compromise a good thing? When isn't it? You might think of the good compromises a married couple makes for one another, or a situation where compromise is necessary in a work team. You might think of situations where compromising on our personal dreams or ambitions is a way of serving others or even of looking after ourselves well. Conversely, you might think of occasions when compromise is not a good thing: when someone abandons an important moral principle, for example, or when only one person in a marriage is always compromising for the other.

2. What gets organized in 12:44-47? The people have already promised to give tithes and contributions (10:32-39), but now officials are being appointed to organize it all (12:44, 47). Similarly, the temple services and song worship get organized (v 45-46).

• **How does this good organization express worship and commitment?** The appointment of officials might seem banal, but it's a vital part of the people's commitment to God. They are figuring out how he actually plugged in the order that he is commanded and get it to work. They are making sure that the temple worship takes place as it is supposed to.

3. How else do the people express their commitment to God (13:1-3)? When the people read from the Scriptures again, they're rocked by what the Lord has said. Ammonites and Moabites are not allowed to be part of the assembly of God. The people immediately take action to make sure that this law is obeyed.

4. What has happened (v 4-5)? There is a chamber in the temple set aside for the resources which the people have brought as gifts to God. Eliashib goes in there, takes all the resources out, and gives the chamber to Tobiah as an apartment.

• **Why is this a bad thing?** First of all, Tobiah is an Ammonite (2:10). He's not even supposed to be in the temple at all. Secondly, we know that he's a non-believer. He's hostile to the people of God (see 2:10, 19; 4:3, 7; 6:1-7). He was a key person in the opposition to Nehemiah's reforms—and he now has a foothold right in the center of the Jewish community. Thirdly, there is now nowhere to store the gifts from the people. Tobiah is preventing them from fulfilling their commitment to God.

5. When Nehemiah finds out about this, what does he do (v 7-9)? Nehemiah gets holy-indignant. He throws all Tobiah's furniture out. Then he has the chamber cleansed and restores it to its intended purpose.

6. APPLY: What are some things that can be like Tobiah in our lives? This could be a person, an activity, even a house or a particular ambition. Anything that causes us to compromise our commitment to God; anything that leads us to directly disobey God's commands; anything that takes up more of our thoughts than God does.

• **What does it look like to deal with those things the way Nehemiah does?** If something is disrupting God's order in our lives, we shouldn't be nice about it. We need to throw it out. We must remove anything that causes us to sin. Then we must ask God to forgive and cleanse us, and reestablish the order which God intended.

7. Next, Nehemiah discovers that more commitments have been compromised. What are they (v 10, v 15-16, v 23)? The people are failing to give the money they promised to those who serve in the temple (v 10), which means that these servants have been forced to leave and find work elsewhere; they are trading on the Sabbath (v 15-16); and they are marrying foreign wives (v 23). These are direct contraventions of the promises they made in 10:30-32.

8. Nehemiah says something about each of these things (v 11, 17-18, 25-27). What do his words reveal about his own motivations and heart? Nehemiah's words reveal his concern for God to be appropriately honored, and for the people's welfare. He says that the house of God has been forsaken (v 11). He says that the people are acting in an evil way and treating something holy with disrespect (v 17)—which could lead to God bringing disaster on them (v 18). He reminds them of their oath not to let their children marry foreign wives (v 25), and gives the example of Solomon, whose faith was compromised because of the influence of his wives (v 26). He describes their marriages as acts of great evil and treachery against God (v 27). He is concerned to help them remain faithful, both for their sake and for God's glory.

EXPLORE MORE
Read 1 Kings 11:1-8
Why did God tell his people not to marry foreigners (v 2)?
God was concerned about influence. Women from other nations who did not worship the Lord would be likely to turn the Israelites' hearts toward other gods.
But why was Solomon tempted to disobey (v 2)?
He loved these women.
How did it become clear that his faith was compromised (v 5-8)?
He began to worship foreign gods himself (v 5) and built shrines to the gods of Moab and Ammon so that his wives could make sacrifices to them (v 8).

9. How does Nehemiah deal with each of these failures?
- **v 11-13** He brings the temple servants and singers back, reinstates the practice of bringing tithes, and appoints reliable treasurers to oversee the distribution of the money.

- **v 19-22** Nehemiah puts in place a hard and drastic stop. He issues an order that the gates of the city have to be closed throughout the Sabbath. He then posts some servants at the gates to ensure that no load can be brought in on the Sabbath. When the traders and merchants spend the night outside Jerusalem in the hope that this situation is just temporary, he threatens them so that they know he is serious.

- **v 25** He confronts the men who have married foreign women, curses them, and beats some of them up. (Note that this is the men he is beating up, not the children or the foreign wives.)

10. What do Nehemiah's prayers in verses 14 and 22 show about his motives? Who does he seek to please?
He seeks to please God alone. He prays these brief prayers as a disposition of trust in the Lord and as a plea for his continued favor.

11. What final things does Nehemiah set right in verses 28-31? He chases away one final enemy, who has allied himself with Sanballat. Then he reestablishes other aspects of the work of the temple.

12. APPLY: What does it look like today to be uncompromising in our passion for the Lord?
- We should be passionate about other people's walk with God. If we have opportunities to teach and lead others in God's ways, we should take those opportunities seriously. If we see people compromising their faith, we should take action to call them back.
- We should seek to please God alone. His honor should be our motivation, not others' opinions. This will have lots of practical implications—for the way we talk about God, the way we think of ourselves, the way we respond to criticism, etc.
- We should be growing in Christlikeness, asking God's Spirit to work in us and through us so that we can represent Jesus to the best of our ability.
- We should be committed and organized. This means putting reliable people around us who will point us to the Lord. It means having regular habits of prayer and Bible reading. For those who have a leadership role, it will mean being diligent in the way we organize church services or small groups.
- We should be passionate about God's mission. We want to see transformation in our cities, in our culture, and in our time.

We want to see people allowing God to
be the lord of their lives. We want to see
God's work of reconciliation, healing, and
rebuilding being done in the lives and
communities around us.

Good Book Guides
The full range

Galatians: 7 Studies
Timothy Keller

Ephesians: 10 Studies
Thabiti Anyabwile

Ephesians: 8 Studies
Richard Coekin

Philippians: 7 Studies
Steven J. Lawson

Colossians: 6 Studies
Mark Meynell

1 Thessalonians: 7 Studies
Mark Wallace

1&2 Timothy: 7 Studies
Phillip Jensen

Titus: 5 Studies
Tim Chester

Hebrews: 8 studies
Michael J. Kruger

Hebrews: 8 Studies
Justin Buzzard

James: 6 Studies
Sam Allberry

1 Peter: 6 Studies
Juan R. Sanchez

2 Peter & Jude: 6 Studies
Miguel Núñez

1 John: 7 Studies
Nathan Buttery

Revelation: 7 Studies
Tim Chester

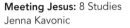

Man of God: 10 Studies
Anthony Bewes & Sam
Allberry

Biblical Womanhood:
10 Studies
Sarah Collins

The Apostles' Creed:
10 Studies
Tim Chester

The Lord's Prayer:
7 Studies
Tim Chester

**Promises Kept: Bible
Overview:** 9 Studies
Carl Laferton

The Reformation Solas
6 Studies
Jason Helopoulos

Contentment: 6 Studies
Anne Woodcock

Women of Faith:
8 Studies
Mary Davis

Meeting Jesus: 8 Studies
Jenna Kavonic

Heaven: 6 Studies
Andy Telfer

Mission: 7 Studies
Alan Purser

Making Work Work:
8 Studies
Marcus Nodder

The Holy Spirit: 8 Studies
Pete & Anne Woodcock

Experiencing God:
6 Studies
Tim Chester

Real Prayer: 7 Studies
Anne Woodcock

Church: 8 Studies
Anne Woodcock

God's Word For You

Galatians For You

"The book of Galatians is dynamite. It is an explosion of joy and freedom which leaves us enjoying a life of blessing. I pray that it explodes in your heart as you read this book."

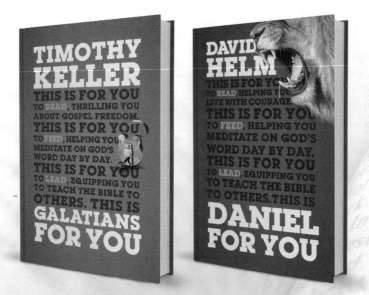

Daniel For You

"The book of Daniel offers you the knowledge that God is still at work, the confidence that it is possible to remain faithful to Jesus Christ, and the strength to live for him in our day."

Find out more about these resources at:

www.thegoodbook.com/for-you

Dive deeper into Nehemiah

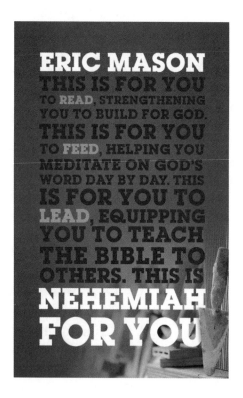

"Nehemiah shows us the work it takes to rebuild representation of God to the nations. We see ourselves in it. But we also see God's intentions, his glory, and his Son."

Verse by verse, pastor Eric Mason unpacks the book of Nehemiah, showing how it points to Jesus and how relevant it is to us today. This accessible and absorbing expository guide can be used for personal devotions, alongside small-group studies, or for sermon preparation.

the good book

C O M P A N Y

BIBLICAL | RELEVANT | ACCESSIBLE

At The Good Book Company, we are dedicated to helping Christians and local churches grow. We believe that God's growth process always starts with hearing clearly what he has said to us through his timeless word—the Bible.

Ever since we opened our doors in 1991, we have been striving to produce Bible-based resources that bring glory to God. We have grown to become an international provider of user-friendly resources to the Christian community, with believers of all backgrounds and denominations using our books, Bible studies, devotionals, evangelistic resources, and DVD-based courses.

We want to equip ordinary Christians to live for Christ day by day, and churches to grow in their knowledge of God, their love for one another, and the effectiveness of their outreach.

Call us for a discussion of your needs or visit one of our local websites for more information on the resources and services we provide.

Your friends at The Good Book Company

thegoodbook.com | thegoodbook.co.uk
thegoodbook.com.au | thegoodbook.co.nz
thegoodbook.co.in